LEVEL 10 LEADER

LEVEL 10 LEADER

Master the 10 Wins to Transform Spirit, Heart, and Mind

Nikhil Tripathi

First Published in 2025

Copyright @ 2025 NIKHIL TRIPATHI

ISBN: 979-8-9924851-4-1

Title: Level 10 Leader

All rights reserved.

The moral right of the author has been asserted.

This book or any portion thereof many not be reproduced or used in any manner whatsoever without the express written permission of the author except for the use of brief quotations in a book review of a scholarly journal.

This book is sold subject to the condition that it shall not, by any way of trade or otherwise, be lent, resold, hired out, or otherwise circulated, without the publisher's prior consent, in any form of binding or cover other than that in which it is originally published.

Disclaimer

This book is a work of non-fiction presented through a fictional narrative. While the leadership principles, frameworks, and insights are based on real-life experiences, the characters, organizations, and events depicted in the story are either products of the author's imagination or are used in a fictional manner for illustrative purposes. Any resemblance to actual persons, living or dead, or real businesses is purely coincidental.

The content of this book is intended for educational and personal development purposes only and does not constitute professional, legal, or psychological advice. Readers are encouraged to exercise discretion and seek appropriate counsel when applying any leadership strategies or recommendations in real-world contexts.

Any references to third-party books, authors, or leadership frameworks are made purely for illustrative and educational purposes. The author claims no affiliation with, endorsement from, or rights to any such intellectual property mentioned within the narrative.

This book is the author's personal passion project. It is not sponsored by, affiliated with, or endorsed by the author's current or past employers, nor by any other organization or institution.

To

Shilpi, Anaya and Ira

for reminding me everyday how blessed I am !

CONTENTS

FOREWORD ix
INTRODUCTION xi
    A. *The 10 Paradoxes of Leadership* 1

Part 1: WINNING THE SPIRIT
    1. *Win With Why* 37

Part 2: WINNING THE HEART
    2. *Win With Who* 65
    3. *Win With Inclusion* 91
    4. *Win With Careers* 119

Part 3: WINNING THE MIND
    5. *Win With Goals* 149
    6. *Win With Growth* 171
    7. *Win With Delegation* 197
    8. *Win With Feedback* 221
    9. *Win With Coaching* 243
    10. *Win With Rewards* 261

Part 4: <u>CLOSING</u>

    B. Another Townhall   *279*

    C. Recap   *297*

AFTERWORD   **303**

Voices of Leadership   **305**

About the Author   **309**

FOREWORD

Having had the privilege of working closely with Nikhil Tripathi over the years, I can attest to his genuine commitment to the leadership principles he shares in *Level 10 Leader*. I have seen him not only implement these strategies but also refine and improve them as he grows in his own leadership journey. His personal evolution as a leader serves as a testament to the effectiveness of the methods he presents, making *Level 10 Leader* not just a collection of theories but a reflection of the author's own lived experience. His growth is a powerful example for anyone looking to develop their leadership skills.

Level 10 Leader differentiates itself from other leadership tools by integrating a wide variety of proven strategies that have been tested and refined over time. From building trust and motivating teams to fostering innovation and embracing change, the author has carefully compiled techniques that are both effective and adaptable. These strategies, drawn from diverse fields and industries, offer practical solutions for any leader seeking to elevate their impact. Each approach is grounded in real-world application, ensuring that readers can implement them with confidence and see tangible results.

One of the powerful features of *Level 10 Leader* is its ability to break down complex leadership concepts into an engaging and relatable story-telling format. By weaving these principles into real-life scenarios, the author makes learning about leadership not only accessible but also enjoyable. Whether you are an experienced leader or just starting your journey, the stories provide valuable insights in a way that resonates with readers at all levels. This narrative approach helps you absorb the key lessons without feeling overwhelmed, making it easier to apply them to your own work and life.

What makes *Level 10 Leader* particularly valuable for teams and organizations is its suitability for group discussion and learning. The stories and leadership strategies provide an excellent foundation for thought-provoking conversations, allowing teams to engage in meaningful dialogue. *Level 10 Leader* encourages readers to reflect on their own leadership styles, challenge assumptions, and exchange ideas with others. Whether used in workshops, book clubs, or team meetings, the book fosters a collaborative environment where leaders can grow together and learn from one another's experiences.

Where time is an invaluable resource, *Level 10 Leader* is worth the investment.

Kim M. Kraus
Retired Senior Vice President Procter & Gamble

INTRODUCTION

The soft hum of a crowded room, the glare of a spotlight, and the steady weight of dozens of eyes watching, waiting. Sarah Thompson stood at the front of the auditorium, clutching the edges of the podium as her voice faltered. The numbers on the screen behind her told a story she wasn't prepared to defend.

Frustration radiated from the audience like heat. The questions started sharp and direct: "Why is your team delaying critical deadlines?" The comments soon became biting: "Do you even know what's causing the bottlenecks?"

And then came the laughter. Quiet at first, but it spread like a ripple across the room.

At that moment, Sarah felt more alone than she ever had.

The Paradox of Leadership

If you've ever been in Sarah's shoes, you know the paradox of leadership. It's a position of pride earned through your hard work and expertise, but it can also feel isolating and overwhelming.

As a leader, you're expected to be confident but humble, people-focused but results-driven, visionary but grounded. You've been recognized for your strengths, but your success depends on your ability to lead, inspire, and empower others—a completely different skill set.

These are the paradoxes that every leader faces, and with the increasing demands of today's workplaces—limited resources, tighter deadlines, and a greater focus on collaboration—there's less room for error.

It's no wonder many leaders feel like Sarah did that day—unsure of themselves and questioning their place.

<u>Your Framework for Leadership Success</u>

But here's the truth: Great leaders aren't born. They're made. More importantly, they choose to be coached into greatness.

This book is your roadmap to becoming the leader your team needs – a Level 10 Leader.

At the heart of this book are three dimensions that every successful leader must master:

1. **<u>Winning the Spirit:</u>** Leadership begins with you. It's about building self-awareness, resilience, and authenticity. Before you can lead others, you need to lead yourself.

2. **<u>Winning the Heart:</u>** Leadership is about relationships. It's about building trust, inspiring your team, and creating a culture where people feel valued and empowered.

3. **<u>Winning the Mind:</u>** Leadership drives results. It's about clarity, strategy, and execution—delivering on goals while balancing the needs of your team.

Within these dimensions are 10 Wins—practical, actionable lessons that will guide you through leadership challenges. From "Winning with Why" to "Winning with Feedback" and "Winning with Coaching," each chapter will equip you with tools and strategies to navigate the paradoxes of leadership with confidence.

INTRODUCTION

How to Read This Book

Congratulations on taking the first step toward becoming the leader your team needs. This book is more than just a guide—it's a journey, a conversation, and a toolkit all in one. To get the most out of it, here's how I recommend you approach it:

1. **Start with the Story**

    Each chapter begins with a story—Sarah's journey as a newly promoted leader. Her experiences are designed to mirror the challenges, triumphs, and paradoxes you may face in your leadership role. As you read, allow yourself to step into Sarah's shoes. Notice how she handles setbacks, navigates relationships, and grows into her role. This isn't just her story—it reflects the challenges you're navigating or may encounter in the future.

2. **Find Your Relevance**

    Leadership isn't one-size-fits-all, and neither is this book. Each chapter contains lessons tailored to different stages of the leadership journey. As you read, pause to ask yourself:

    - **Where do I see myself in this story?**

    - **What parallels can I draw to my own leadership experiences?**

    - **How do these insights apply to my team's needs?**

    You may find certain chapters resonate more than others based on where you are in your leadership journey. That's okay—growth is not linear. Take what's relevant and return to other chapters when the time feels right.

3. **Engage with Reflection Questions**

    Each chapter concludes with reflection questions designed to help you internalize the lessons and explore how they apply to your life and leadership. These questions are not homework—they invite you to think deeply about your purpose, team, and goals. Take your time with them. Journal your responses, discuss them with a trusted colleague, or let them guide your thoughts.

4. **Focus on Implementation**

   Leadership transformation doesn't come from reading alone—it comes from action. The book provides practical suggestions, tools, and frameworks for applying your learning. Treat these as experiments rather than prescriptions. Start small, adapt as needed, and build habits over time. Remember, progress is more important than perfection.

5. **Make It Your Own**

   This book is a starting point, but your leadership journey is unique. Feel free to personalize the strategies, reflect on your experiences, and create your leadership playbook. Growth happens when you take ownership of your development and leverage the lessons here as a foundation for your path forward.

Why This Book? Why Now?

If you're reading this, chances are you're navigating leadership challenges. Maybe you've recently stepped into a leadership role or been leading for a while, but you've hit a plateau. Either way, you're here because you want to grow.

Leadership is never easy. You're managing people, expectations, and results, often all at once. You're learning to lead in a world that demands more adaptability, connection, and clarity than ever before.

This book is here to help.

It's not about lofty theories or generic advice. It's about real-world leadership—practical strategies, relatable stories, and tools you can apply today. It's about helping you navigate the paradoxes of leadership, just like Sarah.

INTRODUCTION

What's Ahead

Over the next chapters, you'll follow Sarah's journey from self-doubt to confidence, from a struggling leader to someone who inspires and empowers those around her. Through her story, you'll learn how to build trust, give effective feedback, coach your team, and more.

You'll see her stumble, learn, and grow like you will because leadership isn't about never failing. It's about learning, adapting, and showing up for your team, no matter what.

By the end of this book, you'll have the tools, confidence, and clarity to lead with authenticity and purpose.

So, let's begin because your journey to becoming a great leader starts here.

> *Great Leaders aren't born; they choose to be coached into greatness!*

CHAPTER A
The 10 Paradoxes of Leadership

Monday, December 2, 10:00 AM – Conference Room, TechInnovate Headquarters

"The Promotion"

TechInnovate's open office buzzed with energy. Nestled in the heart of Silicon Valley, it was a lively hive of innovation. The vibrant colors of the modern design reflected the company's ethos of creativity and collaboration, and the morning sun streaming through the large windows cast a golden glow over the space.

Sarah Thompson, a thirty-four-year-old software engineer, sat at her desk. Her workspace was a mix of meticulous organization and creative chaos—neatly stacked project files sat beside colorful sticky notes, some of which were adorned with encouraging messages from teammates. She glanced at her screen, refining the final slides for the upcoming presentation, her mind already rehearsing the points she needed to hit. Today, she will present the latest software update to TechInnovate's CEO, Jessica Hale.

LEVEL 10 LEADER

Sarah adjusted the lapel of her tailored blazer, her fingers brushing against the necklace her mother had gifted her—a small pendant engraved with *"Dream Big."* This mantra had carried her through long nights of studying, endless debugging sessions, and moments of self-doubt. Today, it felt like a good luck charm.

The team filed into the conference room, where the walls were adorned with motivational quotes and snapshots of the company's latest achievements. Sarah took her place at the head of the table, her heart racing with excitement and nerves. Her manager, Mark, opened the meeting with a brief introduction and then turned the floor over to her.

With steady breaths, Sarah launched into her presentation. She highlighted the software's innovative features, client feedback, and the team's hard work. Jessica Hale, known for her sharp insights and no-nonsense demeanor, leaned forward in her seat, her gaze intense but unreadable. Sarah pushed through the final slide, her voice unwavering.

"Excellent work, Sarah," Jessica said, her tone warm but measured. Your dedication to this project has been truly outstanding.

Sarah felt a swell of accomplishment, but before she could respond, Jessica turned to Mark. "Is this the right time?"

The air in the room shifted, curiosity rippling through the team. Mark nodded, his expression serious.

Jessica stood, commanding attention with her presence. "I have some important news to share. Mark has been chosen to lead our Global Innovations Office, a strategic priority for TechInnovate. His vision has been instrumental in our success, and I have no doubt he'll excel in this new role."

Applause filled the room again, but this time, Sarah felt uncertain.

Who will lead the team now?

Jessica continued, her eyes landing on Sarah. I'm thrilled to announce that Sarah will be promoted to take on Mark's role as Operations Manager. Her technical expertise, commitment, and ability to deliver results make her the ideal candidate for this position."

The room erupted once more, congratulations flowing toward Sarah. She smiled, feeling a rush of pride mixed with disbelief. This was what she had worked so hard for—years of late nights, demanding projects, and proving her capabilities.

"Thank you so much," Sarah said, her voice slightly shaky with emotion. I'm honored and excited to lead this exceptional team.

As the meeting concluded and her colleagues offered handshakes and encouragement, Sarah's gaze drifted to two of her team members—Karen and Tom. Karen's arms were crossed, her smile faint, while Tom avoided eye contact entirely.

A flicker of doubt nudged Sarah. While the moment was celebratory, she couldn't help but notice the subtle tension among her colleagues. *Will they trust me as their leader?* She wondered. But she brushed the thought aside, determined to savor this achievement.

As Sarah returned to her desk, the necklace around her neck felt heavier. The words *"Dream Big"* now resonate differently, not as a motivator but as a reminder of the weight of leadership.

LEVEL 10 LEADER

Monday, January 6, 8:15 AM – TechInnovate Headquarters

"The First Day"

Sarah walked into the office with renewed purpose. The familiar buzz of TechInnovate's open floor plan greeted her, but today, everything felt different. Her usual spot by the window now seemed distant. Instead, she headed toward the larger desk near the corner—Mark's old desk, now hers.

Her footsteps felt heavier, and so did the stares. A few team members congratulated her warmly, offering quick smiles and handshakes. But others were more reserved, their congratulations polite but distant. Tom gave her a curt nod before returning to his screen, while Karen barely acknowledged her.

Sarah reassured herself that it was just an adjustment period. They needed time to adjust to this, just as I did.

She set her bag down and began organizing the desk. Mark had left it spotless, almost impersonal, except for a single note in the center: *"You've got this. They'll follow your lead."* The words were encouraging, but Sarah couldn't shake the pressure they carried.

Her first task as Operations Manager was a team huddle. She prepared carefully, reviewing Mark's notes and outlining her updates. When the time came, she stood at the head of the meeting room, waiting for the team to assemble. Slowly, they trickled in, some chatting quietly, others scrolling on their phones. The energy felt subdued.

"Good morning, everyone," Sarah began, forcing a tone of confidence. "Thank you for being here. I want to begin by expressing my gratitude for the opportunity to lead such a talented team. I know we've been through some changes, but I'm excited about what we can achieve together."

She paused, scanning the room. A few heads nodded, but most remained unreadable.

"I also want to share some quick updates on our current projects," she continued, diving into the agenda. As she spoke, she noticed Karen whispering something to Tom, their expressions hard to decipher. Sarah pushed through, keeping her focus on the slides.

When the meeting ended, Sarah opened the floor to ask questions. The room stayed quiet for an uncomfortably long moment before a junior developer raised his hand to ask about a minor task. The rest of the team shuffled out as soon as the meeting concluded.

Back at her desk, Sarah replayed the huddle in her mind. *What did I miss? Was I too formal? Not clear enough?*

The day passed in a blur of emails, meetings, and project updates, but the underlying tension didn't lift. By the time Sarah wrapped up for the day, she felt exhausted, not from the workload but from the subtle friction she couldn't define.

As she gathered her things to leave, she overheard Karen talking to another team member near the coffee machine.

"Do you think she's ready for this? I mean…… she's great at the technical stuff, but leading a team? That's a whole different ballgame."

Sarah's heart sank. She slipped out of the office unnoticed, the day's weight pressing heavily on her shoulders. Walking to her car, she glanced at her reflection in the building's glass doors. *"Operations Manager"* felt like a badge she hadn't yet earned.

As the sun dipped below the horizon, casting a golden hue over the parking lot, Sarah realized that the initial euphoria of her promotion had already begun to fade. In its place was something heavier: doubt.

LEVEL 10 LEADER

Monday, January 27, 10:00 AM – TechInnovate Headquarters

"Cracks in the Surface"

The first few weeks as Operations Manager were a blur for Sarah Thompson. She poured herself into the role, arriving early, staying late, and meticulously reviewing every detail of her team's work. Her calendar is filled with meetings, deadlines, and strategy sessions. She thought her visible effort would inspire the team, but the cracks in their relationships grew wider.

It started subtly. Karen's questions in meetings became pointed, her tone laced with doubt. "Do you think this new timeline is realistic?" she asked during one team huddle, raising an eyebrow as she scanned the room. A few others murmured in agreement, but no one spoke up directly. Sarah tried to address the concerns diplomatically, but the resistance was palpable.

Tom, meanwhile, had grown more distant. He arrived just on time, left the moment the clock struck five, and avoided eye contact whenever Sarah tried to check-in. One afternoon, she found him lingering in the break room, scrolling on his phone. She approached cautiously, hoping for a casual conversation.

"Hey, Tom. How's QA going on the client app?" she asked with a smile, keeping her tone light.

He barely looked up. "Fine."

"Fine? "Is there anything I should know about?" she pressed.

"Nope," he said flatly, turning back to his phone.

Sarah stood there for a moment, her confidence faltering. She wanted to push further but didn't want to seem overbearing. "Let me know if anything comes up," she said weakly before walking away.

Tension escalated during a one-on-one meeting with Karen. Sarah had asked Karen for feedback on a project timeline, but the response caught her off guard.

"To be honest, I feel like some of these changes are happening too fast," Karen said, folding her arms. We're not accustomed to this level of oversight.

Sarah frowned. "I'm trying to help the team stay on track and avoid surprises. Isn't that what we need right now?"

Karen hesitated, then shrugged. "Maybe. But it feels like we're being micromanaged."

The word hit Sarah like a punch to the gut. "Micromanaged? That's not my intention at all," she said, her voice steady but her chest tightening.

Karen offered a thin smile. "I'm just saying how it feels."

The conversation ended awkwardly, and Sarah spent the rest of the day replaying it. *Micromanaging? Is that how they see me?*

The team's results weren't faring much better. Deadlines were slipping, and client satisfaction scores had dropped. Sarah tried to address the issues in a team meeting, but the room felt heavy with unspoken tension.

"We need to find a way to improve our delivery times," Sarah said, looking around the table. "What's holding us back?"

Karen glanced at Tom, who shrugged but said nothing. Another team member mumbled about the workload, but no one offered concrete solutions. Sarah pushed forward, trying to rally the team, but her words felt like they were hitting a wall.

By the end of the meeting, she felt more disconnected than ever.

LEVEL 10 LEADER

Friday, January 31, 8:30 PM – Sarah's Kitchen, Thompson Residence

"Unravelling at Home"

The strain began to spill into her personal life. One evening, Sarah sat at the kitchen table with Alex, staring blankly at her laptop. "I don't know what I'm doing wrong," she admitted, her voice heavy with frustration. "I've tried everything—listening, collaborating, even giving them space. But nothing seems to work."

Alex reached over and squeezed her hand. "You're trying, Sarah. That counts for something."

"Not enough," she said, shaking her head. Jessica is already noticing the missed deadlines. I don't know what will happen if things don't improve soon."

Alex had no answer, but his steady presence was a small comfort. Still, as Sarah went to bed that night, the weight of the team's doubt and her insecurities pressed down on her like a storm cloud that refused to lift.

Tuesday, February 11, 10:00 AM – Town Hall, TechInnovate Headquarters

"The Silence That Roared"

The main hall of TechInnovate buzzed with anticipation as employees streamed in for the quarterly town hall. Rows of chairs faced the stage, where a large screen displayed the company's latest achievements. Jessica Hale, the CEO, stood at the podium, her confident demeanor commanding attention as the chatter gradually faded.

THE 10 PARADOXES OF LEADERSHIP

Sarah sat near the front with her team, clutching the notepad on her lap. She was eager and nervous—it was her first appearance as the new Operations Manager. Today, she would have to share the team's performance results, a task that felt heavier than she had anticipated.

Jessica began with her usual flair, delivering company updates with clarity and enthusiasm. Her voice carried the weight of leadership, blending optimism with urgency.

"As you know, transparency is a key component of our culture," Jessica said. "We don't shy away from the hard facts because that's how we grow. Today, I've asked each of our functional leaders to provide a candid view of their team's progress."

Sarah's stomach tightened as Jessica continued. After a few other managers presented their updates, Jessica looked toward her and smiled. "Now, let's hear from Sarah Thompson, our newly promoted Operations Manager."

As Sarah stood, the room offered polite applause. She smoothed her blazer as she stepped onto the stage. The spotlight was bright, and the audience's eyes fixed on her. Taking a steady breath, she began.

"Good morning, everyone," she said, her voice clear but tight. "As Jessica mentioned, I'm Sarah Thompson, and I've recently stepped into the role of Operations Manager. I want to start by saying how honored I am to lead such an incredible team."

She clicked the remote, advancing to a slide that displayed metrics for her team's recent performance. The numbers weren't catastrophic—but they lagged expectations.

"I won't sugarcoat it. We've had challenges—missed delivery windows, communication gaps, and some breakdowns in cross-functional coordination. I take full responsibility for where we are. But I also believe in where we're headed."

LEVEL 10 LEADER

She paused, scanning the room.

They're all looking at me like I don't belong up here. Like they're just waiting for me to stumble. If I play it safe, they'll think I'm hiding. If I over-explain, I'll sound defensive. Just say it. Say what you practiced.

"I'm not here today to defend numbers. I'm here to get better. So, I'll ask this directly: If there's feedback—real feedback—not the polite kind—I want to hear it. What are we missing? What's getting in your way? Don't hold back."

Silence.

Not the kind of silence that meant reflection—the kind that meant discomfort.

Sarah's heart thudded in her chest. The quiet stretched long enough to become painful.

Say something. Anyone.

A pen clicked. Someone shifted in their chair. Eyes slid to the side. No one met her gaze.

Oh god. Are they judging me? Or just trying not to be the one who starts something?

Her fingers gripped the clicker more tightly.

Maybe they're afraid. Perhaps they think I won't handle the truth. But that's not me. I can take it. I want to take it.

She took a breath. A deeper one. The kind she had practiced before the mirror.

"Do you believe we're slowing you down?"

Another silence. This one is heavier. A few people blinked. One person scratched their chin. Still, no one spoke.

Sarah felt a strange combination of control and panic.

This is your moment. If you backpedal now, you'll look weak. If you don't push, they'll never speak.

She stepped forward just slightly. Voice firmer now. Clearer.

"Come on. Speak up. Don't do me any favors. I need to know. Give me something."

Something shifted. A flicker across the front row. A shared glance between two directors in the middle. A sharp inhale from somewhere near the back.

Then it broke.

"All right—real feedback?" said a voice from the middle. "Yes. You are slowing us down."

Another followed. "We've had to shift project timelines because we couldn't rely on your handoffs."

"And the quality of deliverables has been inconsistent," someone else added. "We're spending time reworking things that should've been right the first time."

They're really saying this. Out loud. In front of everyone.

Her breath caught. Her feet felt rooted in place. Her smile had vanished.

"It's affecting our clients."

"We're constantly in fire-fighting mode."

"You've got the title, but it doesn't feel like you're in control."

Someone near the back added, "Just being transparent—like she asked."

A low chuckle spread through a pocket of the room.

Sarah tried to speak, but her voice didn't come. Her mouth was dry. Her vision narrowed just slightly.

What have I done?

Jessica rose from her seat and stepped forward, her voice calm but commanding.

"That's enough."

The room stilled instantly.

"This is a forum for solutions—not a pile-on. Sarah asked for feedback, and you've given it. Let's remember who we are as a company."

Jessica turned to Sarah. "Thank you."

Sarah nodded faintly and walked offstage. Her steps were slow, deliberate. She didn't meet anyone's eyes.

The applause that followed was sparse—more habit than support.

As she sank into her chair, her thoughts raced.

I thought courage would be respected. I thought they'd appreciate the honesty. I thought I was ready.

But maybe I'm not.

Tuesday, February 11, 1:00 PM – Washroom, TechInnovate Headquarters

"Shattered Reflection"

Sarah pushed open the washroom door with shaky hands, the muffled sounds of the town hall still ringing in her ears. The harsh fluorescent lights reflected her pale, strained face in the mirror as she gripped the edge of the sink. Her chest felt tight, her breaths shallow.

She turned on the faucet and splashed cold water on her face, hoping to calm the storm inside her. But it was no use. The frustration, humiliation, and overwhelming sense of failure crashed over her like a wave. The voices from the town hall replayed in her mind, sharp and accusatory:

"Your team's delays are hindering our progress."

"Do you even know what's causing the bottleneck?"

"It feels like no one is accountable."

Her vision blurred as tears welled up in her eyes. She sank against the tiled wall, her knees trembling. For weeks, she had been trying so hard—listening to her team, making plans, pushing herself past exhaustion—and nothing seemed to work.

How did it come to this? she thought, her mind racing.

How did I lose their trust so completely?

The door creaked open, and she tensed, quickly wiping her face. But no one came in. She released a shaky breath and pulled out her phone, her fingers trembling as she unlocked the screen. She stared at the home screen for a moment before opening her messages and texting Alex.

Sarah: *"Can you come pick me up?"*

LEVEL 10 LEADER

The response came almost instantly.

Alex: "Of course. What's wrong? Are you okay?"

Sarah: *"No. I just... I need to get out of here."*

Alex: "I'm leaving now. Go to Starbucks and wait for me. You don't need to be there any longer today."

Her phone buzzed again a moment later.

Alex: "We'll figure this out together, Sarah. I promise."

The words brought a lump to her throat. Alex always knew what to say, even when she didn't. She took a deep breath, splashed water on her face again, and straightened her blazer in the mirror. Her reflection stared back at her, pale and exhausted but still standing. *You can fall apart later,* she told herself. *For now, just get out.*

She stepped out of the washroom, avoiding eye contact with colleagues as she made her way to the elevator. The ride down felt interminable, each ding of the floors passing matching the pounding of her heart. When she finally stepped out into the fresh air, she let it fill her lungs and soothe her nerves, if only slightly.

Starbucks was just down the block, a familiar space where she could wait for Alex. She gripped her phone tightly as she walked, her thoughts a jumble of what-ifs and worst-case scenarios. For the first time in her career, she wasn't sure she could fix what was broken, and that terrified her.

Tuesday, February 11, 1:00 PM – Breakroom, TechInnovate Headquarters

"The Breaking Point"

The break room felt heavier than usual, the faint hum of the refrigerator and the clinking of mugs barely masking the tension in the air. Karen sat at the far end of the communal table, her coffee untouched. Tom joined her, his jaw tight as he dropped into a chair. Lisa entered next, her expression drawn, followed by Jake, who hesitated before taking the last seat.

Karen broke the silence, her voice clipped. "Alright, let's address the elephant in the room. That town hall? Completely unacceptable."

Tom snorted, crossing his arms. "Unacceptable doesn't even begin to cover it. She didn't just let us down—she humiliated us in front of the entire company. I'm done."

Lisa shifted uncomfortably, her voice calmer but no less firm. "It was a mess, I agree. But don't you think she was trying to be transparent? Maybe she thought she was doing the right thing."

"Doing the right thing?" Karen snapped. "Transparency is one thing, Lisa, but throwing your team under the bus? That's a whole different story. She didn't even consult us before airing our problems like that."

Mia fidgeted with her mug, her voice hesitant. Perhaps she didn't realize how it would be perceived. She's new to this; she's probably overwhelmed.

Karen leaned forward, her eyes narrowing. "Overwhelmed or not, this isn't about her feelings. It's about the fact that she's making us look bad while we're the ones keeping this team afloat. How long are we supposed to put up with this?"

Tom nodded, his tone grim. "Exactly. It's not just the town hall. It's how she's been running things since day one—micromanaging, questioning every decision, not trusting us to do our jobs. It's exhausting."

Lisa exhaled, glancing at the group. "So, what do we do? Sit around and hope she figures it out?"

Karen's jaw tightened. "No. We can't keep waiting. She's not listening to us, and she's not learning fast enough. This isn't just a bad day—it's a pattern."

Mia looked uncertain. "Are you saying we... what? Go over her head?"

Karen met her gaze, her voice resolute. "Yes. We need to talk to Jessica. This can't go on."

Tom straightened in his chair. "Agreed. Sarah's not ready for this role; we shouldn't have to suffer while she figures it out. Jessica needs to know what's happening."

Lisa hesitated, her brow furrowed. "I don't like the idea of going behind Sarah's back, but... maybe it's the only way. Jessica might be the only person who can help her see what's not working.

Karen nodded firmly. "Exactly. We're not doing this to undermine Sarah—we're doing it because this team deserves better. And if Sarah can't step up, someone else will have to."

Mia's voice was quiet, but her agreement was unambiguous. "Okay. We talk to Jessica."

Karen glanced around the table, her gaze steely. "We go together. We present the facts—calmly and professionally. This isn't personal; it's about the team and the work. Jessica will understand."

The others nodded, their decision cemented. The weight of the conversation hung in the air as they gathered their things and left the break room. Each step back to their desks felt heavier, but for the first time in weeks, they felt a glimmer of control over the situation.

Tuesday, February 11, 1:20 PM – Starbucks, Downtown Palo Alto

"A Familiar Face"

The soft hum of chatter and the rich aroma of coffee greeted Sarah as she stepped into the Starbucks. The space was familiar and calming but felt like a sanctuary today. She found a small table in the corner and collapsed into the chair, setting her bag beside her. The tension in her shoulders refused to ease, and the echoes of the town hall still swirled in her mind.

She ordered a soothing chamomile tea, though she doubted it would work. As she waited, her phone buzzed.

Alex: "Almost there. Hang in there."

Sarah stared at the words for a long moment, her eyes stinging with unshed tears. Alex always had a way of grounding her, but right now, even his support felt like a small lifeline against a rising tide.

"Sarah Thompson?" a familiar voice pulled her out of her thoughts.

She looked up, startled, to see **Michael Carter**, her former mentor, standing by her table. He held a to-go coffee cup in one hand and his laptop bag in the other. Seeing him brought a rush of emotions—relief, nostalgia, and an ache for the stability she'd once felt under his guidance.

"Michael," she said her voice barely above a whisper. "Wow, hi."

Michael's face lit up with a warm smile. "It's been a while. How have you been?" He gestured toward the empty chair across from her. Mind if I sit for a moment?

"Of course," Sarah said, sitting up straighter and wiping her eyes quickly, hoping he wouldn't notice.

Michael set his coffee down and leaned back, studying her with the same perceptive gaze she remembered from years ago. "You don't look okay," he said gently. "What's going on?"

Sarah hesitated, her fingers curling around her tea cup. "It's just... work," she said vaguely, not ready to open up. "You know how it is."

Michael raised an eyebrow but didn't press. "I do. Especially when you're in a leadership role. Let me guess—new responsibilities, high expectations, and a team that's not quite on board?"

She blinked, taken aback by how accurately he'd summed up her situation. "Something like that."

He nodded knowingly. "Been there. More times than I'd like to admit." He glanced at his watch and sighed. "I've got a meeting in a few minutes, but listen, Sarah—if you ever need to talk, I'm here. Seriously. Just reach out."

He reached into his bag and pulled out a business card, sliding it across the table. "You know where to find me," he said.

Sarah took the card, her fingers brushing over the embossed text. "Thanks, Michael. I appreciate it."

Michael stood, giving her shoulder a gentle squeeze. "You've always been one of the sharpest people I've worked with. Don't forget that." With a final smile, he headed for the door.

Sarah watched him leave, the business card still in her hand. A flicker of hope stirred within her, though it was buried beneath layers of doubt and exhaustion. Could Michael help her navigate this mess? Or was she too far gone?

Her thoughts were interrupted when Alex entered the café, his eyes immediately finding hers. The thin facade of composure she'd held onto the moment she saw him crumbled. She stood as he approached, and he wrapped his arms around her without a word.

"Hey," he said softly, his voice steady and grounding. "Let's get out of here."

Sarah nodded against his shoulder, clutching Michael's card as if it were a lifeline.

Thursday, February 13, 2:00 PM – Jessica's Office, TechInnovate Headquarters:

"The Reckoning"

When Sarah arrived at the TechInnovate office after a morning appointment at her daughter Lucy's preschool, it was mid-afternoon. She felt slightly lighter, having enjoyed a brief moment of normalcy with her family. Still, that feeling vanished as soon as she stepped onto the office floor.

The workspace was eerily quiet. Rows of desks sat empty, laptops closed, and chairs pushed in. A sinking feeling settled in Sarah's stomach as she scanned the room. Her team's absence was glaring, and the silence was unnerving.

"Where is everyone?" she muttered under her breath.

Before she could process further, her phone buzzed.

LEVEL 10 LEADER

Assistant: "Jessica wants to see you in her office as soon as possible."

Sarah's stomach flipped. The walk to Jessica's office felt impossibly long. Her mind raced with possibilities, but none of them felt good. When she stepped inside, Jessica was seated at her desk, her expression unusually grim. **John**, the head of HR, sat beside her, his hands folded neatly on the table.

"Close the door, Sarah," Jessica said, her tone calm but clipped.

Sarah obeyed, her heart pounding. "What's going on?" she asked, though she could feel the answer forming in the pit of her stomach.

Jessica sighed, leaning forward slightly. "Your team came to see me this morning—all of them. After the town hall, they felt humiliated and stated that they could no longer work under your leadership."

Sarah's chest tightened, her breath catching in her throat. "They... what?" Her voice was barely a whisper.

"They offered their collective resignation," Jessica continued, her words deliberate. "They feel that you exposed them in an unprofessional and unfair way. They don't believe you have their backs."

Sarah's hands trembled as she sank into the chair across from Jessica. "That wasn't my intention," she said, her voice cracking. I was trying to be transparent and address the issues."

Jessica softened slightly, though her tone remained firm. "I know that, Sarah. But that's not how they perceived it. Perception matters."

John spoke up, his voice measured. "We've asked the team to take the day off and reflect before making final decisions. But

Sarah, you need to think about how to repair this. Currently, their trust in you is severely damaged."

Sarah's mind reeled. The image of her empty office floor, combined with the memories of the town hall, overwhelmed her. "What... what do I do?" she managed to say.

Jessica leaned back, her gaze steady. "To start, take a step back. Give yourself a few days to reflect and regroup. You can't lead effectively when you're running on empty."

John nodded in agreement. "We'll manage things in the short term. But you need time to figure out how to rebuild trust with your team. It won't happen overnight."

Sarah wanted to argue, to insist she could fix this now, but deep down, she knew they were right. She had been running on fumes, pushing herself harder each day, only to find herself further from her team. Her shoulders slumped as she nodded. "Okay. I'll take the time."

Jessica's voice softened. "This isn't the end, Sarah. Leadership is about weathering storms like this. But you need to start by understanding where they're coming from. And then rebuild."

As Sarah left Jessica's office, her emotions swirled—shame, frustration, and a faint glimmer of determination. She returned to her desk, gathered her belongings, and left the office, unsure of what the next few days would bring.

LEVEL 10 LEADER

Wednesday, February 19, 2:00 PM – Conference Room, TechInnovate Headquarters:

"The Apology"

The conference room was stiflingly quiet as Sarah stepped inside. Her team was already seated around the table, their expressions ranging from guarded to openly displeased. Karen sat with her arms crossed, her lips pressed into a thin line. Tom stared out the window, refusing to meet her gaze. Lisa sat near the center, her hands folded neatly, and her eyes were kind but cautious. Ever quiet, Mia had her notebook open but hadn't written a word.

Jessica and John, the head of HR, were at the far end of the table, their presence steady but watchful.

Sarah's chest tightened as she took her seat. She had spent the last 24 hours replaying the town hall events in her mind, feeling the weight of her missteps like a stone in her stomach. Now, faced with her team's discontent, she felt the ground beneath her metaphorically shift.

Jessica cleared her throat, breaking the silence. "Thank you all for attending today. Sarah has requested this meeting to address the concerns you brought to my attention yesterday. Let's keep this discussion honest but respectful."

Sarah swallowed hard, her voice trembling as she began. "I want to start by saying how deeply sorry I am for what happened at the town hall. My intention was never to expose or humiliate anyone. I wanted to be transparent about our current standing as a team, but I realize now that I handled it poorly."

She paused, scanning the room. Karen's expression remained unchanged, and Tom continued to look out the window. Lisa's gaze softened slightly while Mia avoided eye contact, flipping her pen anxiously between her fingers.

"I know I've let you down," Sarah continued. "I've made mistakes, and I take full responsibility for them. I want to rebuild the trust we've lost, but I know that will take time and effort. I'm here to listen and learn from you."

Karen was the first to speak. Her voice was calm but edged with frustration. "It's not just about the town hall, Sarah. It's about feeling like you don't see us as a team. You make decisions without consulting us, and then we're left to clean up the mess."

Her words hit Sarah like a blow, but she nodded. "I hear you, Karen. And I know I need to do better about including the team in decision-making."

Tom finally turned to face her, his expression unreadable. "The town hall was the worst day of my 20-year career," he said flatly. "You didn't just share our struggles—you aired them to the entire company. How are we supposed to recover from that?"

Sarah's throat tightened. "I can't undo what happened, Tom. But I can do everything in my power to support you moving forward. I don't expect forgiveness overnight, but I'm committed to earning back your trust."

Lisa spoke next, her voice quiet but steady. Some of us tried to give you the benefit of the doubt, but it felt like you were speaking about the team, not with us. It hurt because we want this to work, too."

Sarah looked at her, grateful for her honesty and the underlying hope in her words. "Thank you, Lisa. That means a lot. I want it to work, too, and I know I need your help to make that happen."

Finally, Mia looked up. Her voice was barely above a whisper. "I felt exposed. Like my work—and even my learning curve—was on display for people who don't know me. It made me wonder if I even belong here."

The words made Sarah's eyes sting. "Mia, I'm sorry. I should've protected your dignity, not made you feel vulnerable. That's on me."

The room fell into silence again. Jessica leaned forward, her voice calm but firm. "I know emotions are running high, and that's understandable. But I also know this team is capable of incredible things. Trust takes time to rebuild but starts with conversations like this."

She turned to the group. "I trust every person in this room, including Sarah. If I didn't, we wouldn't be having this conversation. I believe we can move forward, but it will require effort from all of us."

John added, "If anyone has concerns about how we proceed, my door is always open. But for now, let's focus on what we can control—our work, communication, and rebuilding our team."

The tension in the room eased slightly, though it was clear the wounds were still fresh. Karen exhaled slowly. Tom tapped his fingers against the table. Lisa offered Sarah a slight nod. Mia quietly closed her notebook.

As the meeting drew to a close, Sarah felt a flicker of hope, though it was quickly overshadowed by doubt. Jessica and John lingered behind, and Jessica placed a hand on Sarah's shoulder.

"Take a few days, Sarah," she said softly. "You need time to regroup. Trust can be rebuilt, but you need the right mindset to do it."

Sarah nodded, her voice barely audible. "Thank you."

As she left the conference room, her heart felt heavy. The storm had passed for now, but the sky was far from clear. And deep down, a small voice whispered a question she couldn't shake:

Am I the right person for this job?

Wednesday, February 19, 7:00 PM – Living Room, Thompson Residence:

"The First Step Forward"

Sarah sat curled up on the couch, her legs tucked beneath her, staring blankly at the television, playing quietly in the background. She was not watching; her mind was elsewhere, replaying the apology meeting over and over. The tension, the hurt in her team's eyes, and Tom's cutting words echoed in her head: *"The town hall was the worst day of my 20-year career."*

The weight of it all pressed down on her. She apologized, took responsibility, and listened to their frustrations, but it was not enough. The trust she had hoped to rebuild was still far out of reach.

Across the room, Gloria moved about the kitchen, the comforting aroma of lentil soup wafting through the air. Alex sat nearby, flipping through a magazine but glancing at Sarah occasionally, his brow furrowed with concern. Lucy toddled over with her favorite storybook, placing it in Sarah's lap.

"Mama, read?" Lucy's small voice broke through the fog in Sarah's mind.

Sarah blinked, forcing a smile as she brushed a hand over her daughter's curls. "Not right now, baby. Maybe Daddy can?"

Lucy pouted but turned to Alex, who quickly scooped her up. "Come on, kiddo. Let us find out what happens next," he said, carrying her to the other side of the room.

Gloria emerged from the kitchen carrying a steaming bowl of soup. "Here, baby. "Eat something," she said, placing it on the coffee table in front of Sarah. "You can't keep running on fumes."

"Thanks, Mom," Sarah murmured, though she did not move to pick up the bowl.

Gloria sat beside her, resting a hand on her shoulder. "You want to tell me what's going on?"

Sarah exhaled shakily. "It's everything, Mom. I feel like I am drowning. My team does not trust me. Jessica asked me to take time off because they threatened to quit. And I just…" Her voice cracked, and she covered her face with her hands. I am not sure if I can fix this.

Gloria's voice was calm and steady, just as it always was. "Baby, I've seen you get through hard times before. You didn't come this far to give up now."

"This feels different," Sarah said, her voice muffled. "It's not just about me anymore. It is about leading a team of people who don't believe in me. How do I recover from that?

Gloria's hand tightened gently on Sarah's shoulder. "You come back by remembering who you are. You have always faced challenges head-on, and this is no different. And sometimes, baby, you need to let someone help you."

Sarah lowered her hands and glanced at Gloria. "Help?" she repeated, her voice uncertain.

"Yes, help," Gloria said. "You've got people in your corner — your family, Jessica, and even those who don't see it yet. But you need to trust someone to guide you. You don't have to do this alone."

Alex chimed in from across the room, bouncing Lucy on his knee. "Your mom's right. You've got to let someone help shoulder the load."

Sarah hesitated, her mind drifting to Michael. She had not yet mentioned her encounter with him at Starbucks, but his words lingered in her mind. *"If you ever need to talk, I'm here."*

"What is it?" Gloria asked, noticing the shift in Sarah's expression.

"I ran into Michael Carter the other day," Sarah admitted. "He was my mentor when I first started at TechInnovate. He offered to help if I ever needed it."

"Well, there you go," Gloria said with a knowing smile. "Reach out to him. What is stopping you?"

"I don't know..." Sarah said, her voice trailing off. "What if he can't help? What if I am beyond fixing?"

Gloria shook her head. "Stop that, Sarah. No one is beyond fixing. And you're not alone in this."

Alex added, "If Michael's offering, it's because he believes in you. Trust that."

Sarah looked between them, her heart heavy but slightly less burdened. She picked up her phone and stared at the screen for a long moment before typing a message.

Sarah: *"Hi Michael, it's Sarah. Are you free for coffee this week? I could use your advice."*

The reply came almost immediately.

Michael: "Sarah! Of course. How about Friday at 10 AM? First coffee's on me."

A faint smile broke on Sarah's face as she looked up at her family. "Friday," she said softly. I am meeting him on Friday.

"Good," Gloria said, her tone resolute. "That's my girl. One step at a time."

As Lucy toddled back over to Sarah with the storybook, Sarah pulled her into her lap, hugging her tightly. For the first time in days, she felt a flicker of hope. It wasn't much, but it was a start.

CHAPTER SUMMARY
The 10 Paradoxes of New Team Leaders

LEVEL 10 LEADER

For Sarah, as for many newly promoted managers, leadership was a journey filled with unexpected challenges. What began as a moment of triumph quickly unraveled into a series of tests that left her questioning her abilities and sense of self. Yet, beneath these struggles lay the deeper forces shaping her experience: **the paradoxes of leadership.**

Though unique to each leader's journey, these paradoxes are universal in their lessons. They demand courage in the face of uncertainty, clarity amid chaos, and resilience in the face of adversity. Sarah's story captures these contradictions, offering a glimpse into the realities of stepping into leadership.

1. **The Paradox of Uncertainty**

    Leadership is a leap into the unknown. Sarah's promotion filled her with excitement but also with an unsettling fear of the unknown. Could she fulfill her new responsibilities?

    - This paradox surfaced on Sarah's **first day** as she tried to engage her team but found herself second-guessing every interaction.
    - It deepened after the **town hall fallout** when uncertainty pushed her to her breaking point.

    Leaders like Sarah must find a way to move forward despite the unknowns. How does one lead confidently when there are no guarantees?

2. **The Paradox of Expectations**

    New leaders face immense pressure to balance competing expectations: delivering results, creating an inclusive culture, and meeting their high standards. Sarah found herself at the center of this tension.

    - Her team's **growing resistance** to her leadership reflected their unmet expectations of her.
    - Meanwhile, Jessica's emphasis on transparency and results at the **town hall** added another layer of pressure.

How can leaders strike a balance between these demands without neglecting their own needs?

3. **The Paradox of Confidence**

   Confidence is a cornerstone of leadership, yet it often feels elusive. Sarah's confidence was eroded by her team's resistance and the harsh feedback from her colleagues.

   - Her self-doubt emerged during her **first team meeting** and deepened when Tom declared the town hall "the worst day of his career."
   - And yet, Sarah understood that true confidence could only come through overcoming these challenges.

   How can leaders build confidence when every misstep feels like confirmation of their inadequacy?

4. **The Paradox of Change**

   Leaders are tasked with driving change, yet change often breeds resistance. Sarah believed her workflow improvements would streamline operations, but her team saw them as micromanagement.

   - Karen's critiques during meetings and the team's collective frustration after the **town hall** highlighted the challenges of implementing change without compromising trust.

   How do leaders manage the delicate balance between progress and resistance?

5. **The Paradox of Time**

   The pressure to deliver results immediately left Sarah with little room to develop the skills she needed to lead effectively.

   - The rushed deadlines and missed client milestones added to her stress, while the **town hall** highlighted the team's growing dissatisfaction.

- Sarah knew that investing time in her leadership growth was essential, but time felt like a luxury she couldn't afford.

How can leaders prioritize long-term growth when short-term demands loom large?

6. **The Paradox of Authenticity**

   Sarah wanted to be transparent and genuine with her team but felt vulnerable whenever she opened up.

   - Her attempt at **straight talk** during the town hall was misinterpreted as exposing her team's flaws, further eroding their trust.
   - Her **apology meeting** felt like a minefield as she struggled to balance honesty and reassurance.

   How do leaders stay authentic without appearing weak?

7. **The Paradox of Privacy**

   Seeking guidance is essential for growth, yet it can feel like admitting failure. Sarah wrestled with this paradox after her chance encounter with Michael Carter.

   - Her hesitation to contact Michael after their meeting at Starbucks reflected her fear of being judged.
   - It was not until her **quiet evening at home** that she found the courage to seek help.

   Why do leaders struggle to admit they cannot do it alone?

8. **The Paradox of Personality**

   Sarah wanted to treat her team members individually but feared inconsistency would undermine her authority.

   - Her interactions with Karen and Tom revealed how challenging it was to tailor her leadership approach without being perceived as favoring one person over another.

   How do leaders strike a balance between consistency and individuality?

THE 10 PARADOXES OF LEADERSHIP

9. **The Paradox of Resources**

   The sheer volume of leadership advice—books, training, mentors—can feel overwhelming. Sarah knew she needed help, but where to start?

   - Her encounter with Michael offered her a potential path forward, though even then, she hesitated.

   How can leaders sift through the noise to find the guidance they genuinely need?

10. **The Paradox of Success**

    The skills that had made Sarah a star individual contributor—her attention to detail and hands-on approach—were now working against her as a leader.

    - Her attempts to control workflows alienated her team, showing that her strengths in execution did not translate to leadership.

    - Sarah began to understand that success as a leader requires an entirely new skill set—one she would have to learn by letting go of habits that had once served her well.

    How do leaders let go of what brought them past success to embrace what is required for their future growth?

PART-1

WINNING THE SPIRIT

CHAPTER 1
Win With Why

"The two most important days in your life are the day you are born and the day you find out why."

— Mark Twain

"Leadership is not about titles, positions, or flowcharts. It's about one life influencing another.

— John C. Maxwell

"Working hard for something we don't care about is called stress; working hard for something we love is called passion."

— Simon Sinek

Friday, February 21, 10:00 AM – The Cornerstone Café, Downtown Palo Alto:

"The Invitation to Look Inward"

Sarah stepped into the cozy café where she had agreed to meet Michael. The rich aroma of freshly brewed coffee wafted through the air, mingling with the hum of quiet conversations and the occasional clink of ceramic cups. It was a haven of calm, a stark contrast to the chaos she had felt inside. She spotted Michael near the corner, seated at a small wooden table with a book open before him.

"Sarah!" Michael's warm voice immediately put her at ease. He rose to greet her with a firm handshake and a smile. "It's good to see you."

"It's good to see you too," Sarah said, managing a faint smile as she set her bag down and took a seat. A barista approached with a tray, placing a cappuccino and a black coffee before Michael. "Thank you," Sarah murmured to the barista, inhaling the comforting aroma of her drink.

Michael grinned. "I took the liberty of ordering for you. You've always been a cappuccino person, right?"

Sarah chuckled softly. "Still am. Thanks for remembering." She took a sip, letting the frothy warmth settle her nerves. For a moment, she felt a sense of grounding. "This is exactly what I needed."

Michael leaned back in his chair, his posture relaxed but attentive. "So," he began, his tone calm and open. "Tell me about your journey so far. What has it been like for you since the promotion? "

Sarah hesitated, her hands tightening around the coffee cup. "Where do I even start?" she muttered, almost to herself. She glanced at Michael, who gave her an encouraging nod, signaling he was listening. She took a breath and began.

"At first, it felt like a dream come true," Sarah said, her voice carrying a mix of nostalgia and disappointment. I worked incredibly hard to earn that promotion—putting in late nights and weekends and pouring everything I had into my projects. When Jessica announced it, I felt like I'd finally made it. My family was so proud. My mom even called all her friends to tell them her daughter was now a manager." She let out a small laugh, but it quickly faded.

Michael smiled softly. "It must have felt amazing to see all your hard work pay off."

"It did," Sarah admitted. "But that feeling didn't last long. I walked into the office on my first day as a manager, and everything shifted. People treated me differently. Karen, who used to be chatty, had become polite and distant. Tom barely spoke to me at all. I kept telling myself it was just an adjustment period, but it never changed."

Michael leaned forward slightly, his eyes steady. "What do you think caused that shift?"

Sarah thought for a moment. "I don't know. Maybe they didn't think I deserved the role. Or maybe I came on too strong. I was so focused on proving I could do the job that I might've... pushed too hard. I started setting deadlines and assigning tasks without checking in with them first. I assumed they'd trust me because we'd worked together before."

Michael nodded, his expression thoughtful but free of judgment. "That's a tough position to be in. What happened next?"

WIN WITH WHY

Sarah sighed, staring into her cup as if searching for answers. "Things just kept... building. Meetings felt tense, even though no one said anything outright. I tried to encourage the team by praising their work, but it always felt forced—like they didn't believe me. And then the town hall..." She trailed off, shaking her head.

Michael waited, letting the silence linger until Sarah was ready to continue. "The town hall was the breaking point," she said finally. "I thought I was honest by sharing our results and asking for input, but it backfired. The entire company called out my team for underperforming. It was humiliating—for them and me. And now... now I feel like I've lost them completely."

Her voice cracked slightly, and she quickly took another sip of her coffee to steady herself.

Michael leaned back, giving her space but keeping his gaze steady. "That must have been incredibly hard," he said softly. "What do you think your team needs from you now?"

Sarah blinked, taken aback by the question. "I... I don't know," she admitted. "They probably just want me to stay out of their way. I feel like anything I do makes it worse."

Michael tilted his head slightly. "And what do you think you need?"

The question hung in the air, heavy with implications. Sarah let out a shaky breath. "I need... clarity. I need to understand why I'm here—why I even wanted this role in the first place. Because right now, I feel like I've completely lost sight of that."

Michael nodded thoughtfully. "Leadership is a lot like steering a ship," he said after a pause. "When the waters are calm, staying on course is easy. But when the storm hits, the captain must focus on the destination, even if the winds are against them. You don't need to control the storm—you need to adjust the sails."

LEVEL 10 LEADER

He let the metaphor sit for a moment, then reached into his bag and pulled out a well-worn book, placing it gently on the table between them. The title, *Start with Why* by Simon Sinek, gleamed in bold letters.

"I want you to have this," Michael said, sliding the book toward her. "It's helped me—and countless others—figure out the deeper motivations behind what we do. Take your time with it. Don't just read it; internalize it. And when you're ready—when you've thought about what this means for you—we'll meet again."

Sarah stared at the book, the weight of the moment sinking in. She managed a polite smile, but inside, her thoughts churned. A book? That wasn't the quick fix she'd been hoping for. She needed answers now, not pages to flip through.

Michael seemed to sense her hesitation. "It's not a quick fix," he said gently as if reading her mind. "But trust me—starting here will make everything else clearer."

Sarah picked up the book, running her fingers over the cover. She still felt uncertain, but Michael's confidence was hard to ignore. "Thank you," she said finally. "I'll… give it a try."

As they parted ways, Sarah stepped out into the crisp afternoon sunlight. The warmth on her face felt almost symbolic, like a small promise of better days ahead. She inhaled deeply, letting the fresh air fill her lungs.

Her thoughts drifted back to what Michael had said about the captain and the storm. She could picture the winds whipping at the sails, the crew looking to their leader for direction. She realized it wasn't about controlling the storm—it was about focusing on the sails and trusting the course ahead.

Maybe that's what I need to do, she thought as she reached her car. *Figure out where I'm going and take it one step at a time.*

With the book tucked under her arm, Sarah felt the faintest glimmer of clarity. It wasn't a solution, but it was enough to steady her for the moment. *I can't calm the storm, but I can steer the ship,* she thought as she drove away, the image lingering in her mind like a quiet reminder of what might come next.

Friday, February 21, 6:30 PM – Dining Room, Thompson Residence

"Unpacking the Questions"

The house was unusually quiet for dinnertime. Alex sat at the table, cutting small pieces of pasta for their three-year-old daughter, Mia, who was arranging the vegetables on her plate into shapes. Sarah sat across from them, her fork poised but untouched. The weight of the day's conversation with Michael lingered, her thoughts circling his questions and advice.

"You've been quiet since you got home," Alex said, glancing up as he handed Mia a napkin. "How did it go with Michael?"

Sarah sighed, setting her fork down. "It was good, I think. Different from what I expected, though."

Alex raised an eyebrow. "Different, how?"

"He was curious—about everything," Sarah said, her voice tinged with a hint of surprise. "He didn't dive straight into advice or try to fix things. He just… asked me a lot of questions. About the team, the town hall, and how I've felt since the promotion. He wanted to know what I was going through."

Alex nodded thoughtfully. "Sounds like he was trying to figure out the full picture before jumping in."

"Exactly," Sarah said, her hands gesturing slightly. "And it worked. I felt like he understood where I was coming from. But then..." She trailed off, a small, uncertain laugh escaping her lips. "Then he gave me a book."

"A book?" Alex echoed, his brow furrowing slightly before a playful smile crept across his face. "That's so Michael."

Sarah laughed, shaking her head. "I know. He said it's about finding my 'why.' Figuring out why I wanted to lead in the first place."

"That sounds... helpful?" Alex offered, his tone half-questioning, half-encouraging.

Sarah shrugged. "Maybe. I was hoping for something more immediate. Like, 'Do this, and everything will magically get better.' A book feels so... slow."

Alex reached across the table, resting his hand over hers. "Sometimes slow is what you need. You've been running at full speed, trying to fix everything simultaneously. This may be your chance to step back and reflect on what truly matters.

Sarah looked down at their hands, her throat tightening. "What if I don't find the answers, Alex? What if I can't fix this?"

"You will," Alex said firmly. "Because you care. You've always cared. That's your strength, Sarah. It's just about figuring out how to show it."

Mia held her plate triumphantly, her vegetables now arranged like a sun. "Look, Mama! I made a sunshine!"

Sarah smiled, a flicker of warmth breaking through her cloud of doubt. "That's beautiful, sweetheart."

Over the next few days, Sarah gravitated toward the book Michael had given her. It started hesitantly—she flipped through the pages quietly at work, skimming a few sentences here and there. But something about the words caught her attention, pulling her in.

One evening, after putting Mia to bed, Sarah curled up on the couch with the book. The house was still; the only sound was the faint hum of the dishwasher in the kitchen. She read about finding purpose and how great leaders inspire by knowing their "why." The words struck a chord, stirring something deep within her.

Her mind wandered to her promotion—the excitement and pride in her mom's voice when she called to share the news. But as the days passed, that excitement had faded, replaced by pressure and doubt. *Why did I want this role so severely?* She wondered. *What was I hoping to achieve?*

At work, she began jotting down thoughts between meetings—scraps of ideas, fleeting reflections. *To prove I'm capable. To support my team. To make my family proud.* The answers felt fragmented and incomplete, but they were a start.

One afternoon, she found herself staring out the office window, Michael's words echoing: *Focus on the sails, not the storm.* For the first time, she allowed herself to imagine what it would feel like to lead with clarity—to know her purpose and let it guide her decisions. The thought was both terrifying and exhilarating.

By the end of the week, Sarah felt a slight but noticeable shift. She didn't have all the answers—not even close—but she was starting to see puzzle pieces fall into place. That evening, curled up on the couch with her notebook beside her, she re-read a passage from the book that had stayed with her all day:

"If we want to feel an undying passion for our work, if we want to feel we are contributing to something bigger than ourselves, we all need to know our WHY."

LEVEL 10 LEADER

The words seemed to leap off the page, resonating like nothing else had. Sarah sat back, the book resting in her lap, as memories and thoughts began to swirl in her mind. She thought about her promotion—the pride she had felt, the excitement of leading a team—and how that had been replaced by self-doubt and a growing sense of isolation.

For weeks, she had been trying to solve the problems around her—her team's disengagement and lack of trust—but she realized now that she hadn't stopped to solve the problem within herself. *Why am I doing this?* The question echoed, not as a doubt but as a call to action.

Her breath quickened as connections formed, pieces of her fragmented reflections falling into place. She grabbed her notebook and started writing furiously, her pen moving faster than her thoughts. Words spilled onto the page: *family, legacy, growth, belonging.* It wasn't perfect—it wasn't even complete—but she felt a spark of clarity for the first time.

Sarah sat up straighter, her heart pounding with excitement and nerves. "This is it," she whispered to herself. "This is what I've been missing."

Grabbing her phone, she quickly scrolled to Michael's number. Her fingers hesitated for just a moment before typing out a message.

Sarah's Text:

Hi Michael, I've had a breakthrough. Can we meet soon? I want to share this with you.

She hit send and stared at the screen momentarily, her thoughts racing. A minute later, her phone buzzed.

Michael's Reply:

That's great to hear, Sarah. How about Monday afternoon? I'm looking forward to hearing what you've discovered.

Sarah set her phone down, a small smile tugging at the corners of her lips. For the first time in weeks, she felt like she was stepping in the right direction—not just fumbling in the dark. She didn't know what Monday would bring but couldn't wait to find out.

Monday, February 24, 2:00 PM – Half Moon Bay, Coastal Lookout

"Steering Toward the Horizon"

Sarah pulled into the small gravel parking lot overlooking Half Moon Bay, the salty tang of the ocean already wafting through her cracked car window. She killed the engine and stared at the waves rolling lazily onto the shore, their rhythmic crash a stark contrast to the constant buzz of Silicon Valley life she was used to.

Why would Michael choose a beach for this? she wondered, stepping out of the car and tightening her jacket against the brisk breeze. A café or an office would have made more sense—something practical and focused. This... this felt different. As she scanned the shoreline, she spotted Michael standing near a cluster of rocks, his hands in his pockets and his face turned toward the horizon.

"Michael," she called as she approached, her voice carrying just enough over the sound of the waves. He turned, his smile warm and easy.

"Sarah! Glad you made it." He gestured to the water. "Beautiful, isn't it?"

"It is," Sarah admitted, though her tone was tinged with curiosity. "Not exactly the kind of spot I expected for a meeting."

Michael chuckled, motioning for her to walk with him along the shoreline. "Well, I thought it might be a good fit for what we'll discuss today. And besides, a little fresh air never hurt anyone."

Sarah stepped beside him, the soft crunch of sand beneath her boots grounding her in the moment. "So," she said after a beat, "why here? What's the connection?"

Michael glanced at her, then nodded toward the water. "You mentioned something last week—a feeling like you were steering a ship through a storm without a compass or a crew that trusted you. I figured a place like this might make that a little easier to picture."

Sarah blinked, taken aback by how clearly he had remembered her words. "I see your point," she said quietly, her gaze following a lone sailboat in the distance. The conversation already felt different—less like a mentor-mentee exchange and more like two people trying to make sense of something bigger.

They walked in silence for a moment before Michael broke it. "So, tell me—what's on your mind? You mentioned in your message that you had a breakthrough."

Sarah exhaled deeply, her breath visible in the chilly air. She clutched her notebook a little tighter. "It came from something I read in the book," she began. "There was a line—it said, 'If we want to feel an undying passion for our work; if we want to feel we are contributing to something bigger than ourselves, we all need to know our WHY.'"

Michael nodded, waiting for her to continue.

"At first, it felt like just another one of those inspirational quotes," Sarah admitted, her words rushing out. "But the more I thought about it, the more it stuck with me. I've been so focused on fixing the problems around me—my team, the results, the expectations—that I haven't stopped thinking about why I wanted this role in the first place. And now... I realize I've completely lost sight of it."

Her voice faltered slightly, but she pressed on. "When I started thinking about my 'why,' it brought me back to my family. My mom worked her whole life, often in jobs that didn't recognize her worth. She used to tell me, 'Sarah, you're going to do something bigger. You're going to leave the world better than you found it.'" She paused, her voice thick with emotion. "I think I wanted this role because it felt like a step toward that goal. But somewhere along the way, I got so caught up in proving I could do it that I forgot what I wanted to do."

Michael listened intently, his expression calm but encouraging. Sarah's gaze turned to the horizon, the sailboats in the distance moving steadily despite the waves.

"I want to be the leader who inspires people—helping them see their worth and potential. I want my team to feel like their work matters, and that they are part of something meaningful. And for myself..." She hesitated, her voice growing softer. "I want to look back someday and know I stood for something real. That I led with purpose, not just pressure."

Michael let Sarah's words linger in the air, the sound of waves filling the silence between them. He glanced toward the horizon, his gaze settling on a small sailboat at a distance. Its sails shifted slightly as the wind picked up, and it rocked gently on the waves.

"Look at that boat," Michael said, pointing. "The captain could be doing one of two things right now."

Sarah followed his gaze, her brow furrowing slightly. "What do you mean?"

Michael tucked his hands into his pockets. "He could be focusing on every little task—the angle of the sails, the tension in the ropes, the speed of the boat. All of that is, of course, important. But if that's all he focuses on, he risks losing sight of the bigger picture when the storm hits."

Sarah tilted her head, curiosity flickering in her eyes. "What's the bigger picture?"

"The destination," Michael said. "The deepest why. The reason the ship is out there in the first place."

He turned to face her, his voice calm but purposeful. "When you lead with tasks alone and focus only on the mechanics, you constantly react to the winds and waves. You get caught up in the day-to-day struggles, trying to fix everything as it comes at you. And when the storm hits, you're so busy trying to control it that you forget why you're even out there."

Sarah nodded slowly, the weight of his words settling on her. "But if the captain focuses on the destination..."

"Exactly," Michael said, his eyes brightening. "If the captain focuses on the destination, they can use it as a compass. Even when the storm is raging, they adjust their course and keep moving toward what matters most. The tasks are still there—they still matter—but they're guided by something deeper. Something that gives them clarity, even in the chaos."

He paused, letting the analogy sink in. "That's what your Why is, Sarah. It's your compass. It's the thing that keeps you steady when everything else feels like it's falling apart."

As Michael's words settled over her, Sarah's eyes fixed on the sailboat. The waves lapped at the shore, their rhythm almost mirroring the churn of her thoughts.

"I get it," she said softly, more to herself than to Michael. "I've been so focused on fixing the sails, pulling the ropes tighter, trying to keep everything moving smoothly... I forgot to think about where I was trying to go."

Michael nodded. "And how do you think that's affected your crew?"

Sarah exhaled sharply, her shoulders sagging. "They've lost trust in me. I've been giving them tasks, deadlines, and feedback, but I haven't shown them why it matters—or why they should trust me to lead them."

Michael took a step closer, his voice gentle but firm. "What would happen if you started leading with your WHY?"

She hesitated, the question hanging in the air like a challenge. "I think…" she began, her voice faltering. "They might finally see that I'm not just trying to control them or meet targets. I care about something bigger—about them, about what we can build together."

Michael studied Sarah's expression as they stood near the beach's edge, the waves lapping gently at the shore. "I can see you're starting to connect the dots," he said, his tone encouraging. "But now the question is—how do you turn that WHY into action?"

Sarah nodded slowly, clutching her notebook. "That's the part I'm struggling with. I know my WHY now—at least, I'm starting to—but I don't know what to do next. How do I demonstrate to my team what this means?

Michael smiled knowingly. "You don't have to figure it all out at once. However, there is a framework that can help you start translating this into something tangible. It's called the **3 Most Important Questions.**"

LEVEL 10 LEADER

Discover Your WHY: The 3 Most Important Questions

01 What experiences do I want to create in my life and leadership?

02 How do I grow into the kind of person who deserves these experiences?

03 What impact will this create for the world around me?

I lead to _____,
so that _____,
and ultimately _____.

Inspired by Vishen Lakhiani's "3 Most Important Questions" framework from The Code of the Extraordinary Mind, which reimagines goal-setting through the lenses of experiences, growth, and contribution.

Visual - 1

WIN WITH WHY

Sarah raised an eyebrow. "What are those?"

"They're questions designed to help you think about what truly matters—both for yourself and the people you lead," Michael explained. He turned toward the water, gesturing toward the horizon where the sailboat had drifted farther out. "Think of these questions as a way to map out not just where you're going but how you'll get there."

He glanced back at her, his expression serious but warm. "Let's go through them."

Michael raised a finger. First, **what experiences do you want to create?** He paused, letting the question settle. "For yourself, for your career—what environment do you want to build? What do you want your leadership journey to feel like?"

Sarah's eyes widened slightly as the question landed. She thought of the tension that had filled her office lately—the guarded looks, the unspoken frustrations. "I want it to feel… collaborative," she said slowly. I want people to trust me and trust each other. Right now, it feels like everyone is just trying to survive."

Michael nodded, a glint of approval in his eyes. "Good. Hold onto that thought."

He raised a second finger. "Next: **How do you want to grow?**" His voice softened slightly. "As a leader and person, what kind of growth do you want to see in yourself?"

Sarah hesitated, then glanced down at her notebook. "I want to grow into someone people believe in," she said quietly. "Not because I have all the answers, but because I'm willing to listen and learn with them. I've been so afraid of looking weak that I've stopped growing."

"That's a powerful realization," Michael said. "Growth isn't about pretending to be perfect—it's about being open to the process."

He raised a third finger. "Finally: **What contributions do you want to make?**" His tone grew more intentional. "What impact do you want to leave behind? For your team, for the company, for yourself?"

Sarah's breath caught slightly, her hand tightening on her notebook. She thought of her Why—the legacy she wanted to build, the desire to create something meaningful. "I want my team to feel like what they do matters," she said, her voice trembling with emotion. "I want them to feel part of something bigger, like their work has a purpose. And for me... I want to know that I've made a difference and helped people grow, not just meet deadlines."

Michael smiled gently, the corners of his eyes crinkling. "Sarah, you're already on the right path. These questions—they're not about having perfect answers. They're about clarity. And clarity starts with you."

Sarah looked at him, her expression a mix of determination and nervousness. "So... what do I do now?"

Michael gestured to the horizon. "Start small. Take a look at the notes you've been jotting down. Use them to remind yourself of your compass—what you stand for, where you're headed. When you start leading with that clarity, it will naturally ripple outward."

Sarah's gaze returned to the sailboat, now a distant speck on the water. The weight of Michael's words settled on her, not as a burden but as a quiet push forward. *I don't have to have all the answers*, she thought. *I need to start.*

As they walked back toward the parking lot, the sound of the waves fading behind them, Sarah felt something stir within her. It wasn't confidence—not yet—but a sense of direction—a faint but steady pull, like a compass pointing her toward something more significant.

"Thank you, Michael," she said as they reached her car. "I don't know how this will turn out, but… I think I'm ready to try."

Michael smiled. "That's all you need to do. Take the first step. The rest will follow."

As Sarah drove away, the horizon stretched out before her, vast and open. For the first time in weeks, she felt like she wasn't just reacting to the waves. She was steering toward something real.

Monday, February 24, 8:00 PM – Living Room, Thompson Residence:

The house was still, save for the soft hum of the refrigerator in the kitchen. Sarah sat at the dining table, a cup of chamomile tea cooling beside her notebook. The table was cluttered with pens, sticky notes, and the book Michael had given her, its cover slightly worn from her constant flipping of the pages.

She stared down at the blank sheet in front of her, the three questions Michael had posed swirling in her mind:

- *What experiences do you want to create?*
- *How do you want to grow?*
- *What contributions do you want to make?*

Taking a deep breath, she picked up her pen and wrote the first question at the top of the page: *What experiences do I want to create?*

Her mind flashed to her office—the strained silence in meetings, the way her team members avoided eye contact. She thought of how she felt walking into the building every morning: tense, guarded, bracing for the day. *That's not what I want*, she thought, not *for me or them.*

LEVEL 10 LEADER

She began writing:

- *A culture of trust and collaboration.*
- *A place where people feel safe sharing ideas and taking risks.*
- *An environment where work feels meaningful and fulfilling—not just a checklist of tasks.*

Sarah paused, tapping the pen against her chin. The words felt good on the page, but they also felt daunting. *How do I even begin to create this?* she wondered.

"Still working?" Alex's voice broke the silence, pulling Sarah from her thoughts. She looked up to see him leaning against the doorway, his arms crossed, a gentle smile on his face.

"Yeah," she said, managing a faint smile. "Just trying to make sense of everything."

He walked over and pulled out a chair across from her. "Mind if I join you for a bit?"

Sarah shrugged. "Sure, but I can't promise this will make much sense. It's... a lot."

Alex reached for her tea and took a sip, earning a small laugh from Sarah. "So," he said, setting the cup back down, "What's on your mind?"

Sarah exhaled deeply, leaning back in her chair. "Michael asked me these questions—these three big, overwhelming questions. And I'm supposed to figure out what they mean for me, my leadership, everything."

Alex nodded. "Sounds like classic Michael. What are the questions?"

She slid the notebook toward him, the questions scrawled at the top. Alex read them silently, then looked back at her. "These don't seem so bad. What's tripping you up?"

WIN WITH WHY

Sarah rubbed her temples. "It's not that they're hard to understand—it's that they're so... big. Like, 'What experiences do I want to create?' How do I even begin to answer that? I'm just trying to get through the day without everything falling apart."

Alex leaned forward, his expression thoughtful. "Okay, but what if you forget about the big picture for a second? Start small. What's one experience you'd want to create—just one—that would make a difference?"

Sarah blinked; his words cut through her overwhelming feelings. "One experience..." she repeated softly. She thought back to her team about how disconnected they seemed. "I want them to feel like they belong," she said. "Like they're part of something bigger. Like they matter."

Alex smiled. "That's a great start. What's next?"

Sarah picked up her pen again, her hand steadier as she wrote the second question: *How do I want to grow?*

This one hit closer to home. She thought about her conversation with Michael, about her realization that she'd been so afraid of looking weak that she'd stopped growing. Her pen moved almost instinctively:

- *I want to be a leader who listens more than she speaks.*
- *I want to grow into someone people trust, not because I have all the answers, but because I'm willing to learn alongside them.*
- *I want to grow into someone who can inspire, not just direct.*

She stopped writing and looked up at Alex. "You think I can do this?" she asked quietly.

He reached across the table, his hand resting over hers. "Sarah, you're already doing this." You care enough to ask the questions—and that's more than most people do. You'll figure it out."

LEVEL 10 LEADER

The last question felt the heaviest. *What contributions do I want to make?* The word "legacy" hovered in her mind, unspoken but ever-present. She thought of her mom, the pride in her voice when Sarah got the promotion, and her family's sacrifices to get her there.

Slowly, she began to write:

- *I want to contribute to my team's growth—not just professionally, but as people.*
- *I want to create something lasting—a culture of trust and purpose that remains even when I'm gone.*
- *I want to make my family proud, not because of what I achieve but how I lead.*

When she finished, she sat back, staring at the page. The answers weren't perfect. They weren't complete. But they felt like a beginning.

Alex glanced at the notebook and then at Sarah. "Looks like you're starting to figure it out," he said with a grin.

Sarah smiled back, a faint glimmer of hope in her eyes. "Yeah," she said softly. "I think I am."

As Alex stood and cleared the table, Sarah remained seated, her eyes fixed on her notebook. The answers stared back at her, imperfect but real. For the first time in weeks, she felt like she wasn't just reacting—she was starting to steer.

Tomorrow, she thought, closing the notebook, *I take the next step.*

BEHAVIORS	ACCIDENTAL MANAGERS	LEVEL 10 LEADERS
What am I GETTING?	• Confusion and burnout from chasing goals without meaning • Disconnected team engagement • Short-lived motivation	• Clarity and focus through purpose • Energized and aligned team • Sustainable drive from within
What am I DOING?	• Reacting to tasks without a clear lens • Saying yes to everything • Leading by urgency, not intention	• Prioritizing based on purpose • Saying yes with intention and no with confidence • Making decisions aligned with values
HOW am I SEEING?	• "Leadership is about proving myself." • "I need to deliver fast, or I'll fall behind." • "Purpose sounds good, but results come first."	• "I lead to serve something bigger than me." • "Purpose fuels performance." • "Clarity of WHY makes the HOW easier."

LEVEL 10 LEADER

The One Thing Challenge – Win with WHY

Answer the 3 Most Important Questions:

1. What experiences do I want to create—for myself and others?
2. How do I want to grow—as a leader and human being?
3. What contributions do I want to make—to my team and the world?

Then, using your answers, craft your personal WHY statement:

"I lead to..."

Write it in one sentence.

Keep it visible.

Let it guide one decision you make this week.

Because when your WHY is clear, your actions have direction—and your leadership has meaning.

Your Next Move

Was this chapter helpful?

If it sparked a new insight or gave you a practical tool, take 30 seconds to leave a quick review.

Your words might be the reason another leader takes the first step.

☞ Leave a review on Amazon

Ready to grow from a reader to a Level-10 Leader?

Unlock Level 10 Leadership Assessment, Workbook and more at resources.level10leader.com

References

1. Simon Sinek, *Start With Why: How Great Leaders Inspire Everyone to Take Action*, Penguin, 2009.
2. Lakhiani, Vishen. *The Code of the Extraordinary Mind: 10 Unconventional Laws to Redefine Your Life and Succeed on Your Own Terms.* Rodale Books, 2016.

PART-2

WINNING THE HEART

CHAPTER 2
Win With Who

"People will forget what you said, people will forget what you did, but people will never forget how you made them feel."

— *Maya Angelou*

"Leadership is not about being in charge. It's about taking care of those in your charge."

— *Simon Sinek*

"People don't care how much you know until they know how much you care."

— *Theodore Roosevelt*

WIN WITH WHO

Thursday, February 27, 10:00 AM – Fire Station, Downtown Palo Alto:

"The Leadership Classroom"

Sarah pulled into the gravel lot of the fire station, her car's tires crunching softly as she parked. The towering red garage doors stood open, revealing gleaming fire trucks lined up inside. Firefighters moved with purpose—some checking equipment, others cleaning gear, and a few chatting in groups. The scene buzzed with quiet intensity, a team constantly preparing for the next emergency.

"Michael sure picks interesting places," she muttered as she exited the car. The smell of smoke and fresh rain lingered in the air, grounding her in the unfamiliar surroundings.

She spotted Michael standing near a group of firefighters gathered by one of the trucks. He waved her over, a broad smile on his face. "Sarah! Welcome to my favorite leadership classroom."

"Let me guess," Sarah said with a smirk. "You're going to tell me firefighting is a metaphor for leadership?"

Michael chuckled. "Not just firefighting—fire stations. Come on, let's take a walk."

Michael led Sarah through the station, pausing occasionally to point out different aspects of its operations. He gestured toward a group of firefighters inspecting their gear. "Take a look at them. Each of these firefighters has a specific role and specialty. They all bring something unique to the team."

Sarah watched as one firefighter meticulously checked a hose for leaks while another adjusted the truck's sirens. "What do you mean by 'specialty'?"

Michael pointed to a nearby firefighter tightening straps on an oxygen tank. "That's Jamie—he's the best under pressure, always stays calm during the toughest calls. Over there? That's Raj—he's our fastest driver and knows every shortcut in the city. And Lisa? She's the strategist, always thinking three steps ahead in a crisis."

Sarah tilted her head, intrigued. "So, the captain has to know all this?"

"Exactly," Michael said. "If the captain doesn't understand their strengths, they can't assign the right person to the right job when it matters most. And more than that, the captain must earn their trust. These people don't just follow orders—they follow someone who truly knows them."

As they walked further into the station, Michael gestured for Sarah to follow him toward a small room with a whiteboard on the wall. "This is where it all comes together," he said, grabbing a marker and writing **Life Timeline** and **DISC** on the board.

"Let's start with the Life Timeline," he began. "Every firefighter here has a story—a timeline of moments that shaped who they are. If their captain doesn't understand those stories, they can't lead them effectively."

Sarah leaned against the whiteboard. "So, I just... ask them about their past?"

Michael nodded. "Ask about their journey. What's been a defining moment in their career? What challenge taught them the most? It's not just about gathering facts—it's about listening and connecting."

Then he drew four letters: **D, I, S, C.** "Now, DISC helps you understand how people operate daily. It breaks people into four styles: Dominance, Influence, Steadiness, and Conscientiousness."

He pointed to the letters as he spoke: "Some people are high-D - direct, results-driven, and always in action. Others might be high-S - steady, calm, and focused on the team. If you're not leading in a way that matches their style, it creates tension."

Sarah furrowed her brow. "So, I need to know their story and style?"

Michael smiled. "Exactly. The Life Timeline tells you *why* they are who they are. DISC tells you *how* they operate. Together, they provide you with the tools to lead them with empathy and strategy.

Michael stepped back from the whiteboard and turned to Sarah. "And there's one more piece to the puzzle—something you've already experienced."

Sarah raised her eyebrows. "You mean the **3MIQs**?"

"Exactly," Michael said. "Think about how it felt when you worked through your 3MIQs last time—when you reflected on the experiences you want, the ways you want to grow, and the contributions you want to make. It gave you clarity, right?"

Sarah nodded. "It did. It was... freeing, almost."

Michael leaned against the whiteboard. "Now imagine giving that same clarity to your team. Ask them about their aspirations. What experiences do they want to have? How do they want to grow? What contributions do they want to make? It's not just about understanding their past and present—it's about connecting with their future."

Sarah crossed her arms, considering. "So, I need to know their past, present, and future."

Michael smiled. "Exactly. It's not just about managing a team—it's about leading people."

LEVEL 10 LEADER

As the alarm bell rang, signaling another call for the firefighters, Sarah watched them spring into action. Each one moved with precision, fulfilling their role without hesitation.

Michael turned to her, his expression serious but encouraging. "When the stakes are high, trust and understanding hold a team together. That's your next step, Sarah: their past, present, and future."

Sarah nodded, her mind racing with questions she wanted to ask her team. "I'm ready to start," she said quickly, her voice brimming with determination. "I want to go back and ask them about their timelines, observe their styles, everything. I need to fix this."

Michael held up a hand, his tone calm but firm. "Hold on, Sarah. That's exactly the mindset you need, but leadership isn't just about doing—it's about preparing. Take some time to reflect first. Look at the books, consider what you've learned here, and plan your approach."

He reached into his bag, pulling out two well-worn books with dog-eared pages. "Here," he said, sliding them across the table.

Sarah picked them up, reading *"The Power of Moments" by Chip Heath and Dan Heath and "Personality Plus"* by Florence Littauer. She turned the first over in her hands. "You really like giving me homework, don't you?"

Michael grinned. "Always. These will help you go deeper. *The Power of Moments* is about understanding the pivotal events that shape people—perfect for building Life Timelines. *Personality Plus* offers a straightforward approach to understanding various personality styles, including the DISC model.

Sarah raised an eyebrow. "No pressure, right?"

Michael chuckled. "Take your time with them. And if you need more, there's always *Drive* by Daniel Pink—it's great for understanding motivation. But let's not overload you just yet."

Sarah hesitated, her eagerness battling against his words. "But what if I wait too long? What if I miss my chance to turn things around?"

Michael stepped closer, his gaze steady. "Your time for action is about to come. But remember—when you act, you need to do it with intention and strategy, not just urgency. Your team will feel the difference."

She exhaled slowly, slipping the books into her bag. "Okay. You're right. I'll take the time to prepare."

Michael grinned, his expression softening. "That's the spirit. Besides, a firefighter doesn't run into a burning building without knowing what's inside, right?"

Sarah chuckled softly, the metaphor hitting home. "You've got a point."

Sarah felt renewed purpose as she stepped out of the station and into the late afternoon sun. *She thought it was time to discover their stories, styles, and dreams. It's the only way forward.*

Thursday, February 27, 8:00 PM – Dining Room, Thompson Residence:

"Reflections in Real Life"

The dining table was scattered with books, notebooks, and a cooling mug of tea. Sarah sat in the soft glow of the overhead light, flipping through *The Power of Moments*. Her pen tapped against her notebook as she read Michael's words from the fire station, echoing in her mind: *"Understand their past, present, and future."*

She looked up from the book, her gaze settling on Alex across the room. He was sitting cross-legged on the floor, focusing entirely on Lily as she worked intently to build an elaborate tower of blocks. Every time it wobbled, he would reach out just enough to steady it, his calm voice encouraging her to keep going.

"High-S," Sarah murmured under her breath, smiling.

Alex looked up, raising an eyebrow. "What was that?"

"Nothing," she said, shaking her head with a grin. But her thoughts lingered. *Steady, dependable, calm under pressure—that's Alex. Always the rock, always making us feel safe. High-S.*

Her gaze softened as she watched them. *If only I could bring that kind of steadiness to my team right now.*

In the kitchen, her mom hummed a tune Sarah recognized from her childhood, the faint clatter of dishes adding a comforting backdrop to the scene. Her mom had flown in when Sarah shared how overwhelmed she felt after the town hall meeting and the fallout with her team.

Sarah's thoughts shifted. *It would be incredible to map out Mom's life timeline.* She leaned back in her chair, allowing her mind to revisit the moments she knew. *She raised four kids on her own after Dad passed. She juggled two jobs while still finding time to coach my soccer team. And now, here she is, helping me—again.*

She jotted down in her notebook:

- **Alex:** High-S (Steadiness)—calm, dependable, family-first.
- **Mom:** Life Timeline—Resilience, Strength, Adaptability.

She paused, staring at the page. The parallels to her team were undeniable. If she could see what drove her family, why was she struggling so much to see the same in her colleagues?

A soft giggle broke her focus. Lily was trying to add one more block to the top of the tower, her tiny hand trembling as the structure swayed. Alex reached out instinctively, steadying her wrist.

"Careful, sweetheart," Sarah called out. "One step at a time."

Alex glanced over, smirking. "You sound like Michael."

Sarah chuckled, realizing he was right. "Guess it's rubbing off."

She returned to her notes, flipping a fresh page in her notebook. Slowly, the questions began to form in her mind, her pen gliding across the page:

- **What's been a defining moment in your career?**
- **What motivates you to do your best work?**
- **How do you want to grow?**
- **What contributions do you want to make?**

"Still working?" Alex's voice brought her back. He had shifted to sit across from her, Lily now asleep on his shoulder. Her small hand clutched his shirt, her chest rising and falling in the steady rhythm of deep sleep.

"Always," Sarah said with a sigh, leaning back in her chair. "But I think I'm starting to figure it out. Michael's right—before I can lead them, I have to know them."

Alex nodded, his expression thoughtful. "You've always been good at understanding people. Look at us—you know exactly what makes me tick."

Sarah smiled faintly. "True. But this feels different. Bigger. If I don't get this right..." She trailed off, her confidence wavering.

"You will," Alex said firmly. "Just take it one step at a time. Like you said to Lily."

Her mom entered the room, drying her hands on a towel. "He's right, you know. Teams don't come together overnight. But with patience—and a little faith—they will."

Sarah let their words settle, the weight on her chest easing slightly. Her pen moved again, this time with more confidence:

- *Understand their stories.*
- *Recognize their styles.*
- *Help them find their dreams.*

Her mom leaned over, placing a gentle hand on her shoulder. "And don't forget, Sarah, you're not doing this alone. You've got people who believe in you."

As she wrote, a sense of clarity began to emerge. She wasn't just building a team but rebuilding trust, one person at a time.

She glanced at Lily, still snuggled against Alex, and whispered, "I can do this. I have to."

Friday, February 28, 8:30 PM – Dining Room, Thompson Residence

"A Message From Lisa"

Sarah glanced at the time on her phone. She sat at the dining table with her notebook open and Michael's books neatly stacked at the edge. Her mom's voice softly hummed from the kitchen, and the gentle sound of Alex reading Lily a bedtime story filled the house, but Sarah's thoughts were far away.

WIN WITH WHO

Her phone buzzed on the table, jolting her from her thoughts. She glanced at the screen, assuming it was another work email or reminder. To her surprise, it was a message from Lisa—the team member who'd always been quietly thoughtful, even amid the recent tension.

Lisa: *Hi, Sarah. I just wanted to check-in. You seemed stressed the other day. I know things have been tough, but they can improve.*

Sarah stared at the message, her chest tightening. Lisa wasn't the type to speak up often, but her words felt sincere, almost like a lifeline. For a moment, Sarah stared at the screen, unsure how to respond. *She believed things could get better after everything that'd happened.*

She let out a breath she didn't realize she'd been holding. The guilt came first—a wave of it. *I should be the one checking in with them, not the other way around.* But guilt was quickly joined by something she hadn't felt in weeks: hope.

With trembling fingers, Sarah typed back:

Sarah: *Thanks, Lisa. That means a lot. I've been thinking a lot lately, trying to figure out how to improve things. I know the team deserves more from me.*

The response came quickly:

"*We all just want to feel like a team again. You've got this, Sarah. Please let me know if there's anything I can do to help.*

Sarah blinked, re-reading the message. The simplicity of Lisa's words shouldn't have felt so profound, but they did. She glanced at her notebook, at the questions she'd been drafting earlier:

- *What's been a defining moment in your career?*
- *What motivates you to do your best work?*
- *How do you want to grow?*

Lisa's message reminded me of what was possible. The team might be fractured, but it wasn't broken—not completely.

She picked up her phone again and opened her messages, typing to Michael.

Sarah: *Hey, Michael. One of my team members just reached out to check on me. It caught me off guard. Does this mean I'm ready to start talking to them? Or should I wait?*

The reply came almost immediately, but instead of advice, it was a question:

"What do you feel ready to do, Sarah?"

Sarah stared at the screen, her thoughts swirling. She hadn't expected the question. She'd been second-guessing herself for weeks, waiting for someone to tell her what to do. But now, as she re-read Lisa's message, she realized she did know—at least a little.

She typed back slowly, thinking through each word:

"I think I need to start connecting with them—one-on-one. I can't fix everything immediately, but if I can understand where they're coming from, maybe I can start rebuilding trust."

Michael's response came a moment later:

"That's exactly where I'd start. Your Why has already guided you here—you want to lead a connected and thriving team. Now it's time to focus on the Who. Start with their stories. Listen more than you talk. When people feel seen and heard, trust begins to grow."

Sarah read the words twice, her chest tightening with emotion. Michael's mention of her Why brought her back to the moment on the beach when she'd articulated her deepest motivations. *A team that's connected and thriving.* She still wanted that more than anything.

"Opening the door," she typed back. *"That's how I'll start."*

"Exactly," Michael replied. *"One-on-one conversations are the most effective way to start. Don't focus on fixing everything. Focus on understanding who they are, what drives them, and what they need from you as a leader. That's where you'll start to see progress."*

Sarah exhaled, her pen hovering over her notebook. She wrote down Michael's words:

- *Why = Lead a connected and thriving team.*
- *Who = Understand their stories, strengths, and dreams.*

She twice underlined "stories, strengths, and dreams" before closing the notebook.

Her phone buzzed once more. It was Lisa:

"Sure, Sarah. Let's talk on Monday."

Sarah smiled faintly, the tension in her chest easing slightly. She didn't know how the conversation would go, but for the first time, she felt ready to try.

Monday, March 3, 2:55 PM – Office Lounge, TechInnovate Headquarters:

"The First Win"

Sarah glanced at the clock: 2:55 PM. She was sitting in a quiet corner of the office lounge, away from the usual hustle. It wasn't a formal meeting room but a space filled with plush chairs and warm lighting—comfortable and inviting. She had chosen it purposefully, hoping it would help ease the tension.

LEVEL 10 LEADER

Her notebook lay closed beside her on the low table, and she gripped her coffee cup tightly. The steam rose in soft spirals, a faint comfort as she waited. *"Listen more than you talk. Start small. Open the door."* Michael's advice looped in her mind.

The sound of footsteps made her glance up. Lisa approached, her usual calm demeanor tinged with hesitation.

"Hey, Sarah," Lisa said.

"Hi, Lisa," Sarah said warmly, gesturing to the chair across from her. "Thanks for making time to meet."

Lisa sat down, her posture guarded. "Of course."

Sarah hesitated, then took a steadying breath. "Lisa, thank you again for your message the other day. It meant more than I can say. Things have been… hard. And I've been struggling to figure out how to rebuild trust with the team."

Lisa gave a slight nod, her gaze softening. "It's been hard for all of us, Sarah. But I know it's not easy being in your position. You've got a lot on your shoulders."

Sarah blinked, momentarily thrown by the unexpected empathy. "Thank you for saying that. I've felt like I've let everyone down—and I don't know how to rectify the situation. If you were in my shoes… what would you do?"

Lisa tilted her head slightly, considering the question. "What would I do?"

"Yeah," Sarah said, leaning forward slightly. You've been here longer than I've. You know this team. Where would you begin if you were trying to rebuild trust and start over?"

Lisa leaned back, her arms crossing thoughtfully. "Honestly? I'd start fresh. Wipe the slate clean and get to know everyone again. What makes them tick? What do they care about? Trusting someone is hard when you don't feel like they know you."

Sarah nodded slowly, the weight of Lisa's words sinking in. "That's an excellent idea. Starting fresh."

She paused, then added, "Would you be open to starting with me? Maybe we could... share. About where we've come from and what's shaped us. Nothing formal. Just a conversation."

Lisa hesitated, then smiled faintly. "Sure. I think that's something we could both use."

The two of them shared stories over coffee for the next hour. Sarah discussed her years as a software developer and how stepping into leadership felt like entering a world she hadn't fully understood. Lisa shared about her chaotic project at her last company, where stepping into a leadership role—even unofficially—had taught her the value of clear communication.

They laughed over small anecdotes—Sarah's first disastrous attempt at public speaking and Lisa's penchant for color-coded spreadsheets. Slowly, the layers of formality and tension began to peel away, giving way to a genuine connection.

As their conversation wound down, Lisa glanced at her watch, surprised. "Wow, I didn't realize how much time had passed. This was... nice."

"Agreed," Sarah said, her smile reaching her eyes for the first time in weeks. "I didn't think I'd feel this good after a meeting."

Lisa chuckled. "Same here. Honestly, I wouldn't mind continuing this. Maybe we could pick it up tomorrow?"

"I'd love that," Sarah said, a flicker of excitement in her voice. "It feels like we're just getting started."

"Then let's do it," Lisa said, standing. "Same time tomorrow?"

"Same time," Sarah confirmed, standing as well. "Thanks, Lisa. For being open to this."

"Thanks for asking," Lisa replied, smiling before heading out.

Back at her desk, Sarah replayed the conversation in her mind. For the first time in weeks, she felt lighter, more grounded. Lisa's words stayed with her: *"It's hard to trust someone when you don't feel like they know you."*

She opened her notebook and jotted down:

- *Start fresh.*
- *Understand their stories.*
- *Keep building the connection.*

It wasn't a solution to everything, but it was a start. And for now, that was enough.

Wednesday, March 12, 3:30 PM – Break Room, TechInnovate Headquarters:

"The Seed of Trust"

Sarah and Lisa have met regularly for the past week, carving out pockets of time for uninterrupted conversations. Their discussions have shifted from small anecdotes to more profound reflections about their strengths, challenges, and what truly motivates them. Each meeting feels lighter and more manageable—like two colleagues rediscovering their shared purpose.

In their latest meeting, Sarah leaned back in her chair, listening as Lisa described a moment from her childhood that shaped her collaborative nature.

"My dad always said, 'The world doesn't move forward unless people work together,'" Lisa said with a laugh. "It stuck with me. That's why I always step in when people struggle to connect."

"That explains so much," Sarah said warmly. "You're the glue that holds this team together."

Lisa blushed slightly but didn't argue. "What about you, Sarah? What inspired you to lead?"

Sarah hesitated, then smiled. "Honestly? It wasn't my plan. But I've realized I'm here because I want to create something lasting that makes people feel valued and seen."

Lisa nodded thoughtfully. "You're starting to do that, you know."

Sarah blinked, surprised by the statement. "You think so?"

"Yeah," Lisa said firmly. These talks mean something." At least to me."

Later that afternoon, Sarah dialed Michael's number, a rare moment of nervous excitement bubbling in her chest. When he answered, his tone was as warm as ever.

"Sarah! How's it going?"

"It's... good," Sarah said, almost surprised by her words. "I've been meeting with Lisa frequently. She's opening up in ways I didn't expect, and I'm finally starting to understand what makes her tick."

"That's great to hear," Michael said. "It sounds like you're making progress."

"I think so," Sarah said. "But I know it's just one step. The rest of the team is... well, it will take more time."

Michael's voice softened. "And that's okay. Leadership isn't about rushing to fix everything but laying the groundwork.

What has worked with Lisa might not work with Karen or Tom, but you're building the skills you need to adapt.

Sarah exhaled, a weight lifting from her chest. "Thanks, Michael. I needed that."

"Keep going," Michael said. "You're on the right path."

Later that week, Lisa sat across from Karen and Tom in the break room, nursing a cup of tea. The air was thick with unspoken tension.

"I've been meeting with Sarah a lot," Lisa began, glancing between them. "And I have to say… she's trying. She is."

Karen scoffed softly, folding her arms. "Trying doesn't fix what happened."

"I know," Lisa said calmly. "But she's listening. She wants to understand us as individuals, not just as a team.

Tom leaned back, his expression skeptical. "She can listen to all she wants, but actions speak louder than words. Has anything changed?"

Lisa hesitated, searching for the right words. "Not yet. But I think it's coming. She's figuring it out."

Karen shook her head. "I'll believe it when I see it."

The conversation concluded on a tense note, leaving Lisa caught between hope and frustration. While she trusted Sarah's intentions, she knew convincing Karen and Tom wouldn't be straightforward. She reflected that this would take time and headed back to her desk.

Back in her office, Sarah stared at her notebook, the pages filled with scribbled notes and reflections. Lisa's words replayed in her mind: *She's figuring it out.* It wasn't a victory, but it was progress.

One step at a time, she reminded herself, closing the notebook. *One team member at a time.*

Thursday, March 13, 2:00 PM – Huddle Room, TechInnovate Headquarters:

"The Conversation That Mattered"

Sarah sat at her desk, the ticking clock growing louder in her ears as the minute hand crept toward 2:00 PM. She had spent the morning preparing for this meeting—not with notes or plans, but with herself. *Stay calm. Listen. Don't defend. Just open the door,* she reminded herself.

The knock came precisely on time. Sarah straightened, smoothing her hands over her notebook before calling out, "Come in."

Tom entered, his frame filling the doorway. His expression was neutral, his jaw set. He nodded briefly before sitting in the chair across from her desk, folding his arms tightly across his chest. Everything about him screamed *I don't want to be here.*

"Thanks for coming, Tom," Sarah began, her voice steady but soft. "I appreciate you making time."

Tom shrugged, his gaze flickering around the room before settling over her shoulder. "Sure."

The silence that followed felt as thick as a knife. Sarah's heart thudded in her chest as she leaned forward slightly, keeping her hands visible and open on the desk. "I wanted to meet because things haven't been easy lately. For you, for the team, for me. I want to understand what's on your mind."

LEVEL 10 LEADER

Tom's eyebrows twitched downward, a faint frown settling on his face. "What's on my mind?" He let out a dry laugh, shaking his head. "You really want to know?"

"I do," Sarah said firmly. "Whatever it is, I'm here to listen."

Tom's gaze snapped to hers, sharp and appraising, as if he were deciding whether she meant what she said. Finally, he leaned back in his chair, arms still crossed. "Okay. What's on my mind? The town hall, for starters. That was a mess. And since then? The team's been stuck in neutral. No direction, no trust. It's frustrating, Sarah. Really frustrating."

Sarah took a steadying breath, watching Tom shift in his seat. "You're right," she began, her voice calm but firm. "The town hall didn't go the way I wanted. And since then, I've been trying to find my footing—to find a way to move forward. But I know I've fallen short."

Tom tilted his head slightly, his gaze narrowing. "It's not just about falling short. It's about trust. I've been here 20 years, Sarah. I've seen leaders come and go, and I've seen what happens when they lose sight of the team."

"Twenty years," Sarah repeated, letting the weight of his words settle between them. She leaned forward slightly, her gaze steady. "That's an incredible legacy, Tom. You've seen this team through so many ups and downs. I can hardly imagine the depth of knowledge and experience you bring.

Tom blinked, visibly taken aback. His shoulders relaxed just a fraction. "Well... yeah. I've been around long enough to see how things work."

"And that's exactly why I need you," Sarah said earnestly. "You know what works, what doesn't, and what this team needs. I can't rebuild trust without learning from you."

Tom shifted in his seat, his arms uncrossing slightly. "You're putting a lot on me."

Sarah smiled faintly. "Not on you alone. But you're someone the team looks up to, Tom. They trust you. That makes your perspective invaluable to me."

Tom exhaled, rubbing the back of his neck. "Look, Sarah. I'm not sure if this can be fixed. But... I'll admit, I respect the fact that you're trying. That's more than I can say for some leaders I've seen."

Sarah felt a flicker of relief, her chest loosening. "Thank you, Tom. That means a lot to me."

Tom hesitated before giving her a slight nod. "But let's be clear. It will take more than words to rebuild trust. You're going to have to show us."

"I understand," Sarah said. "And I'm not asking for instant trust. Just... a chance to start earning it."

Tom nodded again, his posture loosening further. "All right. We'll see."

As Tom left the room, Sarah leaned back in her chair, letting out a long breath she hadn't realized she was holding. His words replayed in her mind: *"They trust you. That makes your perspective invaluable."*

It wasn't a breakthrough, but it felt like a shift. She opened her notebook and wrote:

- *Keep listening. Trust takes time.*

For the first time in weeks, the knot in her chest loosened. *She thought one inch at a time*, a faint smile curving her lips.

LEVEL 10 LEADER

WIN WITH WHO

BEHAVIORS	ACCIDENTAL MANAGERS	LEVEL 10 LEADERS
What am I GETTING?	• Surface-level cooperation • Resistance, silence, or disengagement • A team that delivers tasks but withholds trust	• Deeper connection and commitment • Candid feedback and honest conversations • A team that feels seen, heard, and valued
What am I DOING?	• Talking more than listening • Treating everyone the same • Focusing only on outcomes and tasks	• Learning each person's story, style, and strengths • Leading with empathy and curiosity • Investing time in personal conversations
HOW am I SEEING?	• "They work for me." • "People are here to do their jobs." • "Staying distant helps me stay professional."	• "I work for my team." • "Everyone has a story, and I want to understand it." • "Strong relationships drive strong results."

The One Thing Challenge – Win with WHO

Pick one team member. Have an honest conversation—not about tasks, but about them.

Ask any of these questions:

- "What's a story that shaped who you are?"
- "How do you like to be supported when things get hard?"
- "What's something you care about outside of work?"

Don't script it. Just be curious.

Then listen—fully.

Because leadership starts with connection.

Connection starts when someone feels seen.

Your Next Move

Was this chapter helpful?

If it sparked a new insight or gave you a practical tool, take 30 seconds to leave a quick review.

Your words might be the reason another leader takes the first step.

☞ Leave a review on Amazon

Ready to grow from a reader to a Level-10 Leader?

Unlock Level 10 Leadership Assessment, Workbook and more at resources.level10leader.com

References

1. *Heath, Chip, and Dan Heath. The Power of Moments: Why Certain Experiences Have Extraordinary Impact. Simon & Schuster, 2017.*

2. *Littauer, Florence. Personality Plus: How to Understand Others by Understanding Yourself. Revell, 1983.*

3. *Pink, Daniel H. Drive: The Surprising Truth About What Motivates Us. Riverhead Books, 2009.*

4. *Lakhiani, Vishen. The Code of the Extraordinary Mind: 10 Unconventional Laws to Redefine Your Life and Succeed on Your Own Terms. Rodale Books, 2016.*

5. *Irvine, G. (2015). Teacher, Leader, Mentor. American Jails, 29(1), 72-73.*

CHAPTER 3
Win With Inclusion

"Diversity is being invited to the party; inclusion is being asked to dance."
— *Verna Myers*

"Diversity is a fact, but inclusion is a choice we make every day. As leaders, we have to put out the message that we embrace and not just tolerate diversity."
— *Nellie Borrero*

"You don't build a culture of inclusion with checklists. You build it by leading with humility, curiosity, and courage."
— *Brené Brown (paraphrased)*

Tuesday, March 18, 10:00 AM – Michael's Kitchen

"Back to Another Fire Station"

Sarah stepped into Michael's kitchen and was immediately struck by its inviting warmth. The aroma of fresh herbs and roasted vegetables filled the air, and various colorful ingredients were laid out neatly on the counter.

"Welcome to my lab," Michael said with a grin, gesturing around the kitchen. "Today, we're cooking up something special."

Sarah raised an eyebrow, her curiosity piqued. "Cooking? I thought this was supposed to be one of your coaching sessions."

"It is," Michael said, handing her an apron. "But today, we're trying something a little different. Trust me—it'll all make sense soon."

As Sarah tied the apron strings, she glanced at the ingredients: vibrant red tomatoes, fresh basil, garlic, a block of Parmesan, olive oil, and various spices. "So... what are we making?"

"A simple pasta dish," Michael said, handing her a cutting board and a knife. "But before we start, let me ask you—what makes a dish great?"

Sarah frowned thoughtfully. "The ingredients, I guess? Freshness, quality..."

"Absolutely," Michael said. "But let me ask you this: If I served you a plate of plain boiled pasta or just a bowl of raw tomatoes, would you call it a great meal?"

Sarah chuckled. "No. That's not a meal. That's... ingredients."

"Exactly," Michael said, his voice shifting to a more serious tone. Many people believe that leadership is about having the right ingredients—a diverse team with various skills, backgrounds, and perspectives. And while diversity is important, it's not the whole story. Inclusion is what happens when you bring those ingredients together in the right way to create something extraordinary."

Sarah paused, letting the metaphor sink in as Michael continued. "Think about it. Each ingredient has its unique flavor and purpose. Garlic brings depth. Tomatoes bring acidity. Olive oil binds it all together. If you don't balance them carefully, the dish doesn't work. Too much of one thing—or not enough of another—and the whole experience falls apart."

He picked up a handful of fresh basil and held it out to Sarah. "Take this basil. On its own, it's fragrant and sharp. But combining it with everything else makes it part of something greater—a symphony of flavors."

Sarah nodded slowly, her mind churning. "So, it's not just about having the ingredients—it's about how you use them."

Michael smiled. "Exactly. Inclusion isn't just about diversity—it's about creating an environment where every individual, every person, feels essential and valued. That's when you go from a collection of parts to something magical."

As Michael moved to chop the garlic, he glanced at Sarah. "So, take a moment to think about your team. Who are your ingredients?"

Sarah blinked, momentarily startled by the question. She leaned against the counter, letting her mind drift to her team. "Well," she began slowly, "there's Lisa. She's the steady one—the voice of reason when things get chaotic."

Michael nodded approvingly. "Steady, like olive oil. It doesn't demand attention, but it ties everything together."

Sarah smiled faintly. "Then there's Tom. He's… experienced and a bit skeptical, but he knows this team and the work inside out. He has this depth of knowledge that's hard to replace."

"Ah, like garlic," Michael said, his knife halting for a moment. "Strong, sometimes sharp, but essential for flavor. What about Karen?"

Sarah hesitated, feeling her chest tighten slightly. "Karen is... complex. She's talented, no doubt, but she's also guarded. I think she's still waiting to see if I'm worth trusting."

"Like a spice, you're not quite sure how to use yet," Michael said thoughtfully. "When handled right, spices like that can elevate a dish. But they can overpower everything else if you don't approach them carefully."

"And Mia," Sarah added, her voice softening. "She's quiet but incredibly creative. When she speaks up, it's usually something brilliant."

"Like a touch of Parmesan," Michael said with a grin. "Doesn't always take center stage, but it makes everything better when it shows up."

As Michael stirred the sauce, Sarah stared at the ingredients before her. For the first time in weeks, she felt a flicker of hope. Her team wasn't a collection of problems to fix—they were a mix of unique qualities waiting to be brought together.

"Do you see it now?" Michael asked, his voice breaking into her thoughts. "Inclusion isn't just about recognizing these traits—it's about creating an environment where they can thrive together.

Sarah nodded slowly. "I see it. But... it's going to take work."

Michael smiled. "All good recipes do. But you've got the ingredients, Sarah. Now, it's time to start cooking."

Sarah straightened, her mind still whirring with the metaphor. "Okay, I get it. We have a recipe for cooking this meal. But what about a recipe for building an inclusive team? How do I bring these 'ingredients' together?"

Michael set down the spoon and turned to face her. "Great question. And the answer isn't as simple as following a recipe. Building an inclusive team isn't about a fixed formula but behaviors. The actions you take every day set the tone for inclusion.

He gestured toward the ingredients on the counter. "Let's keep cooking, and I'll walk you through six key behaviors that create a culture of inclusion. You're already familiar with them—they're the reason this meal will come together.

Michael handed Sarah a handful of fresh basil. "Let's start with **curiosity**. Smell this."

Sarah held it to her nose, inhaling the sharp, fragrant aroma. "It's amazing."

"Curiosity is the same," Michael said. "It's about noticing the unique qualities of each ingredient—or person—and wanting to learn more about them. When you're curious about your team's stories, strengths, and perspectives, you create an environment where they feel valued and understood."

Sarah thought of Lisa. "I guess I've already started with Lisa. I asked her about her journey, and it helped us connect."

Michael nodded. "Exactly. Keep doing that, not just with Lisa but with everyone."

He pointed to the saucepan, where the tomatoes were bubbling away. "Now, **empathy**. These tomatoes are acidic. On their own, they're harsh. But when we add a pinch of sugar, it balances the flavors."

Sarah picked up the sugar and sprinkled it in, watching the sauce transform. "So empathy is like sugar—it softens the edges?"

WIN WITH INCLUSION

Michael smiled. "Yes. Empathy is about understanding what someone might be going through and responding in a way that helps them feel supported. It's how you show your team that their experiences matter."

Sarah thought of Karen and Tom. "I need to work on that with some of my team members. I've been so focused on results that I've forgotten their feelings."

Michael handed her a wooden spoon. "Now stir."

Sarah hesitated. "What if I mess it up?"

"Exactly!" Michael said with a laugh. "That's **humility**—admitting you don't have all the answers and being okay with learning as you go. Leadership isn't about being perfect; it's about being open."

As Sarah stirred, she smiled. "I suppose I've been doing that too. It felt vulnerable when I told Tom I was still learning, but it was the right thing to do."

"Humility is what makes you approachable," Michael said. "And that's essential for inclusion."

Michael turned to the stove, taking the saucepan off the heat. "Next up is **courage**. Sometimes, you have to take bold actions, even when they're uncomfortable."

He reached for a jar of chili flakes and sprinkled them into the sauce. "Like adding spice. It's a risk, but it makes the dish come alive when done right."

Sarah chuckled. "I guess the town hall was my 'chili flakes' moment. It didn't go as planned, but I was trying to do something bold."

"And that's the key," Michael said. "Courage isn't about always getting it right. It's about showing up and trying again."

He placed the pot back on the stove. "Now, **ownership**. This is your sauce. You're responsible for how it turns out, not the tomatoes, basil, or garlic. You."

Sarah nodded, her expression serious. "As a leader, I must take responsibility for the team's culture. I can't wait for them to come around—I must lead the way."

Michael smiled. "Exactly. Ownership isn't about blame—it's about taking initiative to improve things."

Finally, Michael picked up a wedge of Parmesan and handed it to Sarah. "And **allyship** is the finishing touch. It's about supporting and advocating for others, especially those who might feel overlooked."

As Sarah grated the cheese over the sauce, she thought of Lisa. "So, it's not just about creating a space for people—it's about standing with them."

Michael nodded. "When you show someone they belong, you amplify their voice. And that creates a culture where everyone feels valued."

Michael wiped his hands on a towel and reached into his bag, pulling out a thin booklet. He slid it across the table toward Sarah. "This is a resource from Catalyst. It outlines six key behaviors for fostering inclusion: curiosity, empathy, humility, courage, ownership, and allyship.

Sarah picked it up and read the title, *"Getting Real About Inclusive Leadership.* "This looks perfect. It's exactly what I need right now."

Michael smiled. "Use it as a guide, not a checklist. And here's one more suggestion: Start keeping an inclusion journal. Write down your experiences with these behaviors. What worked? What didn't? Where can you improve? The journal will help you stay intentional and celebrate progress."

Sarah nodded, her determination growing. "Curiosity, empathy, humility, courage, ownership, allyship—and now a guide to help me put them into practice." Thank you, Michael. I feel like I'm finally starting to see the path forward."

Michael grinned. "You are. Remember, progress is not perfection. It's just like cooking, Sarah. Start with what you have, and keep refining as you go."

As Sarah left, the comforting aroma of the finished dish lingered in the air. The session had been more than a lesson—it had been a revelation. She felt ready to start creating something extraordinary, one behavior at a time.

Wednesday, March 19, 9:30 AM – Conference Room, TechInnovate Headquarters:

"The Recipe for Inclusion"

The small conference room buzzed softly as the team settled into their seats. Sarah stood at the head of the table, her notebook and the Catalyst report sitting neatly in front of her. She had intentionally left the whiteboard blank, not wanting to assume the team was ready for what she had to share.

As she glanced around the room, Sarah noticed the varied expressions. Lisa smiled warmly, always the emotional anchor. Sitting near the end, Mia was quiet as usual, her eyes flicking between Sarah and the blank whiteboard. Tom leaned back in his chair, arms crossed, exuding his familiar skepticism. Karen sat tightly folded, her gaze laser-focused on the whiteboard, already wary of where this might go.

Sarah took a deep breath and began. "First, I'd like to express my gratitude for taking the time to be here. I know we're all busy, and I don't take it for granted that you showed up."

She hesitated briefly, softening her tone. "I called this meeting because I've been reflecting a lot on how we work together as a team and how I've been showing up as your leader. I know I haven't always gotten it right. I'm still learning. But I want to do better and believe we can grow together."

The room remained quiet. Tom raised an eyebrow, and Lisa offered a supportive nod. Karen's posture stayed stiff, and Mia tucked a strand of hair behind her ear, still silent.

"I've been learning about some behaviors that support inclusion—things I believe could genuinely benefit our team," Sarah continued. "But before I share anything, I want to ask: are you open to hearing about it? I don't want to assume. I promise this won't be a lecture."

The silence hung for a moment.

Lisa broke it. "I think it's great that you're reflecting on this, Sarah. I'd love to hear what you've learned."

Mia nodded slightly, then spoke softly. "Yeah… I'm open. I think it could be helpful."

Tom leaned back further in his chair. "I'll hear you out. Just keep it practical—I'm not here for another fluffy leadership workshop."

Sarah smiled faintly. "Fair enough, Tom. This is grounded, I promise."

Karen sighed audibly but finally spoke. "As long as this doesn't mean more meetings or busy work, I'll listen."

"Thank you," Sarah said sincerely. "I appreciate your honesty. Let me show you what I've been working on."

Introducing the Framework

Sarah walked to the whiteboard and picked up a marker. "These are six behaviors I've been learning about. They're actions that help build an inclusive culture."

She began writing:

1. Curiosity
2. Empathy
3. Humility
4. Courage
5. Ownership
6. Allyship

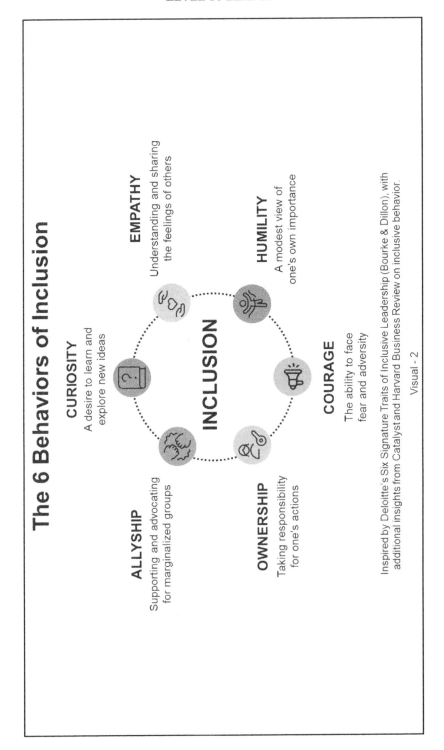

WIN WITH INCLUSION

Turning back to the team, she said, "These six behaviors fall into two categories: Leading Inwards and Leading Outwards."

She drew two columns on the board and labeled them:

- Leading Inwards: Curiosity, Empathy, Humility
- Leading Outwards: Courage, Ownership, Allyship

"'Leading Inwards' is about self-awareness and personal growth—understanding ourselves and building stronger connections. 'Leading Outwards' is about action—creating a culture where everyone feels valued and supported."

Sarah paused and added, "I'll be honest—I'm still learning about these myself. But I'd love for us to explore them together."

Sarah opened her notebook. "For example, curiosity is about asking questions and really listening to the answers. I've been trying to practice that more with all of you."

Lisa smiled. "I've noticed. It's made a difference."

"Thank you, Lisa," Sarah said warmly. "Empathy is about understanding what others might be going through and responding with care. Humility is admitting I don't have all the answers—which has been tough, but I'm working on it."

She turned to the team. "But I don't want this to be just me talking. I'd like us to learn these together. And to do that, I'd like to ask for your help."

"What if we each chose one behavior to explore in more depth?" Sarah suggested. You could think about what it means to you and how it applies to our team and share your perspective in a future meeting. There is no pressure—just your thoughts."

The room was quiet for a beat.

Lisa spoke first. "I'd love to take curiosity. Asking questions is something I enjoy, so this feels like a good fit."

LEVEL 10 LEADER

Tom leaned back, arms still crossed. "Fine. I'll take courage. Seems like a challenge, and I don't mind those."

Karen folded her arms tighter. "Ownership. But don't expect a PowerPoint from me."

"That's all I'm asking," Sarah said. "Your voice."

Mia glanced at the board and then looked at Sarah. "I'll take allyship. I care about it, but I don't always know what it looks like in practice."

Sarah nodded. "That's a perfect place to start. And I'll take humility."

"Thank you, everyone," Sarah said. "I know this is different. Not everyone's sold on it yet—and that's okay. This isn't about being perfect. It's about making progress together."

As the team stood to leave, Lisa lingered.

"I think this was a good idea, Sarah. It feels like a fresh start."

Sarah smiled. "Thanks, Lisa. That means a lot."

Reflection

As Sarah packed up her notebook, she felt a quiet sense of relief—and hope. She had invited her team into the process, and they had stepped forward—even Karen, in her own guarded way.

She thought one behavior at a time—one step at a time.

WIN WITH INCLUSION

Thursday, March 20, 12:00 PM – Cafeteria, TechInnovate Headquarters

"A Different Flavor"

The cafeteria hummed with its usual midday energy as Lisa, Tom, Karen, and Mia settled into a corner table. Trays of half-eaten sandwiches, steaming cups of coffee, and brightly colored salads cluttered the space.

Tom tore open a packet of chips and leaned back in his chair. "So, does anyone else feel like we've been part of a leadership experiment lately?" His tone was light, but his words lingered.

Lisa smirked as she sipped her coffee. "You mean Sarah's sudden deep dive into 'inclusion behaviors'? Come on, Tom, admit it—you're at least a little intrigued."

Tom shrugged. "Intrigued? Maybe. Sold on it? Not yet."

Mia spoke quietly, her gaze fixed on the table. "She's... different. Like, actually different. Did you notice how she asked before sharing that framework in the meeting? That felt respectful. New."

Karen poked at her salad with her fork and scoffed faintly. "Sure, she's trying. But we've all seen these leadership trends before. Give it a month, and we'll be back to sprinting for deadlines without a check-in."

Lisa raised an eyebrow. "I don't think it's a phase. Sarah's been consistent. Vulnerable, even. That takes guts—not just ideas."

Tom nodded slightly. "That part about humility hit differently. For her to stand there and admit she doesn't have all the answers... that's not the Sarah we met six months ago."

Karen didn't respond right away. She kept her eyes on her tray but didn't challenge the point. Mia offered a soft smile. "I think she's trying in a way that matters this time."

Tom leaned forward, folding his arms on the table. "Okay, but this whole 'pick a behavior' thing? I still don't know what to say about courage. What am I supposed to do—give a TED Talk?"

Lisa laughed. "You don't have to be a hero. Just talk about what it means to you. That's the point."

Mia added, "I've been reading about allyship. It made me realize how often I stay quiet when someone's being overlooked. It's uncomfortable—but now I notice it."

Karen finally spoke, her tone less sharp. "The ownership thing? I'll admit it makes sense. If we want a better team, we can't expect Sarah to fix everything. We're part of it."

Tom raised an eyebrow. "Wow. Karen's going soft."

Karen rolled her eyes but allowed a faint smirk. "Don't get used to it."

Lisa grinned. "Come on, you chose ownership. You've got this."

Tom lifted his water bottle. "All right. Here's to progress, not perfection."

Lisa smiled and tapped her cup against his. Mia followed, her eyes bright with quiet resolve. Karen hesitated, then lifted her bottle and clinked it gently with the others.

"To progress," she said, just loud enough to hear.

The conversation shifted to lighter topics as the group returned to their lunches. But beneath the surface, something had shifted—just slightly: cautious optimism, a willingness to try.

And sometimes, that was more than enough.

Thursday, March 27, 10:00 AM – Conference Room, TechInnovate Headquarters

"We, The Team"

The small conference room buzzed with quiet anticipation. Sarah sat with her team at the table, and the whiteboard behind her displayed the six behaviors: curiosity, empathy, humility, courage, ownership, and allyship. Unlike previous meetings, she chose to sit among the group rather than at the head of the table—signaling that this was not a presentation but a conversation.

"Thank you all for your effort in exploring these behaviors," Sarah began. "This isn't about being perfect—it's about learning together. Think of it as a team effort, like we're putting puzzle pieces together."

She looked around, her tone encouraging. "Who wants to start?"

Lisa raised her hand. "I'll go. Curiosity is about asking questions that open up conversations. One thing I found interesting was how it can prevent misunderstandings."

Tom leaned back, arms crossed. "Like when you flagged that last-minute change in the rollout timeline a few weeks ago? I was ready to move forward, but your question helped us catch a flaw."

Lisa smiled. "Exactly. That was curiosity in action."

Tom raised an eyebrow. "So how do we build that into how we work? Not just wait for someone to speak up?"

Lisa paused. "Maybe we set aside five minutes at the end of every meeting for open questions—anything we've overlooked or want to understand better."

Mia nodded gently. "That could help people like me who need a little time to process before jumping in."

Mia continued. "Empathy stood out to me too. It's not just understanding what someone's going through—it's about doing something about it."

Lisa smiled. "Like when I saw you buried in tasks last month and took over the presentation prep. You didn't even ask—I just knew."

Karen, uncharacteristically soft, added, "That kind of check-in... we could all do more of that. Just a simple 'How are you holding up?' would go a long way."

Sarah nodded and jotted on the board:

- Normalize checking in with teammates.
- Make support visible, not assumed.

Sarah cleared her throat. "Humility really resonated with me. It's about being honest and open to learning when I don't have the answers."

Tom smirked. "Like when we pushed back on the project schedule, and you actually changed it instead of defending it?"

Sarah smiled. "Exactly that. It wasn't easy, but it was the right thing."

WIN WITH INCLUSION

Lisa chimed in. "We could build on that—celebrate wins, even small ones, and make it okay to admit mistakes."

Karen crossed her arms, then nodded. "And it shouldn't just come from you, Sarah. We all need to acknowledge each other."

Sarah added:

- Celebrate wins, big and small.
- Encourage peer recognition.

Tom leaned forward, more reflective now. "Courage sounds simple—'speak up'—but it's more than that. It's knowing when and how to do it."

Lisa smiled. "You've never had trouble speaking up, Tom."

Tom chuckled. "Yeah, but there's a difference between being blunt and being helpful. Like when Mia called out the unrealistic timeline with a better plan. That was courage."

Mia looked surprised but pleased. "I only spoke up because I knew you'd listen."

Sarah turned to the board:

- Frame feedback constructively.
- Focus on solutions, not just issues.

Karen sighed but spoke with a thoughtful edge. "Ownership? It's not just about doing your part—it's about owning the culture we're building here. All of us."

Tom nodded. "Like when you proposed that new documentation process after the deadline fiasco. That was ownership."

Karen shrugged, but her tone softened. "I just wanted to fix what wasn't working. But yeah... I guess that's what it looks like."

Lisa added, "Maybe we hold each other to that standard—name it when we see it."

Sarah wrote:

- Hold each other accountable.
- Fix things together, not in silos.

Mia's voice was quiet but sure. "Allyship was eye-opening for me. It's about making sure no one feels invisible."

Lisa nodded. "Like when Sarah brought up my idea in the client meeting—it had been brushed aside, but she circled back to it."

Sarah added gently, "Allyship is about amplifying voices, especially the ones that don't always get airtime."

Tom leaned in. "Let's make a pact—if someone gets interrupted or overlooked, we speak up."

Karen nodded, surprising even herself. "Yeah. Everyone deserves to feel seen."

Sarah captured it on the board:

- Amplify overlooked voices.
- Call out interruptions constructively.

Bringing It All Together

Sarah stood and reviewed the board, now filled with ideas:

- **Curiosity:** Add five minutes for open questions at the end of meetings
- **Empathy:** Normalize checking in during high-stress times

- **Humility:** Celebrate wins and encourage peer recognition
- **Courage:** Deliver feedback with solutions, not just critiques
- **Ownership:** Share accountability and fix issues together
- **Allyship:** Amplify quieter voices and stop interruptions respectfully

"Thank you, all of you," Sarah said, her voice warm. "This felt real. But I'd love to know—was this helpful? Anything that surprised you?"

Lisa smiled. "Honestly? It felt different. Not a training. More like… us, figuring things out."

Tom nodded. "Didn't expect much when this started, but I'll admit—it felt grounded."

Mia added, "I appreciated the space to share. It felt collaborative, not top-down."

Karen leaned back, then said simply, "I felt heard. That doesn't always happen."

As the team packed up, the energy in the room shifted. Sarah remained in her seat, watching them leave—each one a part of the fabric she was beginning to weave together again.

She opened her notebook and wrote:

> *One behavior at a time. One inch at a time. One heart at a time.*

Then she smiled—because it wasn't just movement.

It was momentum.

LEVEL 10 LEADER

Saturday, July 29, 12:30 PM – Cozy Café, Downtown

"A Family That Eats Together"

The warm scent of freshly baked bread and roasted vegetables filled the cozy café as Sarah walked in, accompanied by Alex and her mom, Gloria, by her side. Michael was already seated at a corner table, looking over the menu with a relaxed smile.

"There she is," Michael said warmly, standing to greet Sarah with a firm handshake. "The one who's been weathering storms and steering the ship."

"Barely steering," Sarah replied lightly, sliding into her chair. "More like bailing water."

Alex grinned, pulling out her chair. "And doing it with more grace than you'll admit."

Gloria chuckled as she took her seat beside Sarah. "She always downplays it, but we see it. Every late night, every hard decision—it's all part of the journey."

Michael nodded. "And it's a journey you're walking with courage. Not everyone takes the time to reflect and grow, Sarah."

As the server brought over their drinks, the conversation softened. Gloria poured water into her glass and turned to Sarah. "I've seen you at your lowest over the past few weeks, sweetheart: the tears, the doubts, the exhaustion. And I've also seen you pick yourself up time and again. That kind of resilience isn't easy."

Sarah glanced at her mom, her throat tightening. "It's been… a lot. Some days, I wasn't sure I'd make it through."

WIN WITH INCLUSION

Alex reached for her hand, his touch grounding. "But you did. And you didn't do it alone. You've leaned on us, and that's what we're here for. You don't have to carry it all by yourself."

Michael leaned forward slightly. "And don't forget the strength it takes to lean on others. That's leadership too, Sarah—knowing when to ask for help."

Sarah took a deep breath, looking around at the people who had stood by her. "It's hard to see the progress sometimes. I feel like I'm still figuring out so much. But the team… they're starting to trust me, at least a little. And I'm starting to trust myself."

Michael smiled. "From what I've heard, you're doing more than starting. Your work—introducing the inclusion behaviors and creating space for your team's voices—is not small, Sarah. It's transformative."

Gloria's eyes glistened. "And it's transforming you too, my girl. I've seen it in the way you carry yourself and the way you talk about your team. You've found your purpose again."

Alex nodded. "You've been more grounded and thoughtful. Even when you're exhausted, there's a spark in you. That spark is what's lighting the way for your team."

Sarah looked down at her drink, her voice trembling slightly. "I just… I want to do right by them. I want to be the leader they deserve."

Michael's tone was steady and kind. "And you are. Not because you have all the answers but because you're willing to listen, learn, and lead with heart. That's what makes great leaders."

Gloria placed a gentle hand on Sarah's shoulder. "You've always had heart, Sarah. Now you're showing the world what it can do."

LEVEL 10 LEADER

Alex raised his glass, a warm smile spreading across his face. "To Sarah—the leader we're all proud to know."

Michael lifted his coffee cup. "To progress, not perfection. And to the courage it takes to keep moving forward."

Gloria clinked her glass softly against Sarah's. "To the journey—and the woman walking it with grace."

As their glasses clinked, Sarah felt a wave of emotion she couldn't hold back. Tears welled in her eyes, not from sadness but from her overwhelming gratitude and love for the people around her.

"I wouldn't have made it this far without you," she said softly. "All of you."

Michael smiled. "That's what a good crew does—lift the captain when the seas get rough."

Gloria reached over and squeezed Sarah's hand. "And you'll keep going, sweetheart. One step, one inch at a time."

As the conversation shifted to lighter topics, Sarah let the warmth of their encouragement settle in her heart. The road ahead was still uncertain, but for the first time, she felt steady. She wasn't just leading her team—she was leading herself.

And that, she realized, was the true victory.

WIN WITH INCLUSION

BEHAVIORS	ACCIDENTAL MANAGERS	LEVEL 10 LEADERS
What am I GETTING?	• Groupthink and silence in meetings • Hidden disengagement or discomfort • A culture of compliance, not contribution	• Diverse ideas and open dialogue • Stronger problem-solving through varied perspectives • A culture where everyone feels they belong
What am I DOING?	• Favoring familiar voices • Overlooking quiet contributors • Making inclusion a one-time event or policy	• Seeking out different views intentionally • Rotating who speaks first or leads • Practicing curiosity, humility, and allyship
HOW am I SEEING?	• "Inclusion is HR's job." • "If no one complains, things must be fine." • "Treating everyone the same is fairness."	• "Inclusion is my daily leadership habit." • "Silence may mean someone doesn't feel safe." • "Equity means giving people what they need to thrive."

The One Thing Challenge – Win with INCLUSION

Pick one behavior from the list below—and practice it with intention this week.

- **Curiosity** – Ask someone, "What's one thing I don't know about your experience here?"
- **Empathy** – Notice someone's silence. Check-in privately: "How are you, really?"
- **Humility** – Say, "I might be missing something—what do you see that I don't?"
- **Courage** – Speak up when someone is being interrupted, dismissed, or overlooked.
- **Ownership** – Ask, "Whose voice is missing from this decision?" and help bring it in.
- **Allyship** – Publicly appreciate someone whose contributions are often undervalued.

Pick just one. Practice it. Reflect on the impact.

Inclusion isn't a project.

It's a habit—built one behavior, one moment, one leader at a time.

Your Next Move

Was this chapter helpful?

If it sparked a new insight or gave you a practical tool, take 30 seconds to leave a quick review.

Your words might be the reason another leader takes the first step.

☞ Leave a review on Amazon

Ready to grow from a reader to a Level-10 Leader?

Unlock Level 10 Leadership Assessment, Workbook and more at resources.level10leader.com

References

1. Catalyst. *Getting Real About Inclusive Leadership*. A resource highlighting six key behaviors to foster inclusion, collaboration, and innovation.

2. Brown, Brené. *Dare to Lead: Brave Work. Tough Conversations. Whole Hearts.* Random House, 2018. A powerful exploration of courage and vulnerability in leadership.

3. Edmondson, Amy. *The Fearless Organization: Creating Psychological Safety in the Workplace for Learning, Innovation, and Growth.* Wiley, 2018. A guide to fostering psychological safety and collaboration.

CHAPTER 4
Win With Careers

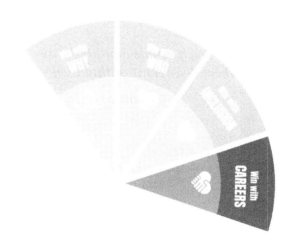

"People don't grow in roles; they grow through experiences."

— *Marcus Buckingham*

"You can't teach people anything. You can only help them discover it within themselves."

— *Galileo Galilei*

"Do what you love, and you'll never work a day in your life."

— *Confucius*

Monday, April 7, 9:00 AM – Grandview Community Theater, Downtown

"The Scene Behind the Scene"

The dimly lit theater buzzed with quiet activity. On stage, a group of actors rehearsed their lines, their voices echoing softly in the spacious area. Sarah stepped into the aisle, her heels clicking against the wooden floor, as Michael waved her over from the director's table near the front row.

"Welcome to the creative chaos," Michael said with a grin, gesturing toward the stage. "Take a seat. You're about to see what real collaboration looks like."

Sarah slid into the chair beside him, curious. "Chaos? Looks more like a debate."

Michael chuckled. "Exactly. Watch closely—it's the kind of debate that makes magic happen."

The actor stood mid-stage, flipping through a worn script, while the director leaned against a prop table. They were rehearsing a key scene from *Hamlet*—the confrontation between Hamlet and Gertrude in Act III.

"This line," the actor said, pointing to the script, "where Hamlet says, 'You go not till I set you up a glass where you may see the inmost part of you'—I get the anger, but it feels incomplete. It's almost as if he's trying to save her."

The director raised an eyebrow. "Save her? That's interesting. Why do you think that?"

The actor hesitated, then began pacing. "Because he's not just accusing her. He's pleading with her to see the truth, to change. There's frustration, sure, but there's also hope."

LEVEL 10 LEADER

The director nodded thoughtfully. "I like that. What if we lean into that hope? Perhaps you could lower your voice here instead of shouting, making it almost a whisper. What do you think?"

The actor stopped pacing, his eyes narrowing in thought. "If I do that, it might make the later anger hit harder. The quieter I am here, the more explosive it feels when he loses control."

"Exactly," the director said, her eyes lighting up. "Let's try it. But let's not decide too quickly—if it doesn't work, we'll tweak it together."

As the rehearsal wrapped up, Michael turned to Sarah. "What do you think?"

"It was fascinating," Sarah said. "But I feel like there's more to unpack."

Michael nodded, standing and gesturing toward the exit. "Let's grab a coffee. Some lessons make more sense when we discuss them out loud."

A short walk later, they entered a small café adorned with black-and-white photographs of old theater performances. The cozy atmosphere offered a stark contrast to the bustling energy of the rehearsal. Sarah slid into a booth across from Michael, her cappuccino steaming.

Michael leaned back in his seat, sipping his black coffee. "What did you take away from what we just saw?"

Sarah frowned thoughtfully. "They weren't just running the scene but building it up. Each of them brought something different to the table. The actor had this emotional insight, and the director helped refine it into something bigger."

Michael nodded. "Exactly. The director could have easily chosen to direct the scene—told the actor exactly what to do, how to deliver the lines, and where to stand. It would have been fine but not extraordinary."

Sarah tilted her head. "So, what made it extraordinary?"

Michael gestured to the stage, recalling it in his memory. "Because it wasn't just her vision. It was theirs. By partnering with the actor, the director uncovered something richer and more authentic than she could have done alone."

He leaned forward, his tone softening. "But here's the thing, Sarah. Co-creation like that doesn't just happen out of thin air. It's built on a foundation."

Sarah's curiosity deepened. "What kind of foundation?"

Michael smiled. "Trust and safety. The director knew the actor's strengths and motivations—that's **Win with Who**. She also created an environment where the actor felt safe enough to share his ideas—that's **Win with Inclusion**. Without those two, co-creation becomes fake or forced."

Michael paused, letting the words settle. Then he asked, "Now, here's the real question: How can this approach be applied to a career conversation between a manager and an employee?"

Sarah's brow furrowed as she considered the question, her mind already beginning to draw parallels. "Well... I guess a career conversation could go two ways. The manager could inform the employees of their next steps—what role they should aim for and what skills they need to develop."

Michael nodded. "That's one way. But what's the alternative?"

Sarah leaned forward, warming to the thought. "The alternative is what we just saw—a conversation. The manager asks questions, listens, and builds on the employee's wants. Instead of saying, 'This is what you should do,' it's about asking,

'What do you want? What excites you? What's your vision for yourself?'"

Michael's eyes gleamed. "Keep going."

Sarah continued, her voice growing stronger. "And then, the manager doesn't just agree or disagree—they add to it. Perhaps the employee has a significant goal but doesn't see how their current role relates to it. The manager helps them bridge that gap. Together, they create a path that aligns the employee's aspirations with the organization's goals."

Michael leaned back, smiling. "Exactly. Career co-creation is about partnership. And like we saw in the theater, it's built on trust and inclusion. Without those, it's just empty advice."

Sarah sat back, letting the idea settle. "It makes so much sense. When I think about my team, I've spent a lot of time figuring out their next steps on my own. But maybe I've been looking at it the wrong way."

Michael nodded. "It's not just about figuring it out—it's about working together. And when you do, the results will surprise you."

Monday, April 14, 10:00 AM – Mentor's Lounge, The Horizon Building, Downtown:

"Canvas and Conversation"

Sarah stepped into the quiet, sunlit mentor's lounge. The room was lined with bookshelves filled with titles on leadership, innovation, and personal growth. A long table occupied the center, scattered with papers and a whiteboard on one end. Michael was already there, leaning over a set of colorful templates in front of him.

"Sarah!" Michael greeted her warmly. "I've got something to show you that might help with your question from the other day."

Sarah smiled, pulling up a chair. "You mean how to co-create careers without fumbling?"

Michael chuckled. "Exactly. You've nailed the why and the what of co-creation. Now, let's discuss the how. I've got a framework and a tool that I think will make things clearer."

Michael slid a template toward Sarah, a large Career Canvas sheet with sections for goals, skills, experiences, and opportunities.

"Let's start with the first step: **Connect.**" Michael tapped the top-left section labeled *'Aspirations.'* "The first thing you want to do is understand the person sitting across from you. What drives them? What do they want to achieve?"

He handed her a marker. "Let's say you're talking to Lisa. What would you write here?"

Sarah frowned thoughtfully. "Lisa wants to grow into a project lead role. She has mentioned that she enjoys organizing and motivating others."

"Perfect," Michael said. "Now, ask yourself: what's the deeper why? What about leading excites her?"

Sarah hesitated. "I'm not sure... I'd need to ask her."

"Exactly," Michael said with a grin. "That's the point of **Connect.** Start by asking open-ended questions and listening. Use the canvas to capture what they say."

Michael pointed to the section labeled *'Opportunities.'* "Once you've connected and understood their aspirations, move to the second step: **Collaborate.** Here, you're exploring how their goals align with the team and organization's needs."

LEVEL 10 LEADER

He picked up a marker and wrote: *'Lead a new client project.'* "For Lisa, this could mean taking on a stretch assignment where she gets to practice leading without the full responsibility of a formal role."

Sarah tilted her head. "So this is where we brainstorm together? She shares her ideas, and I share mine?"

"Exactly," Michael said. "You're co-creating possibilities. Think of it as a Venn diagram: her aspirations and the organization's needs intersect with each other. Your job is to find the overlap."

Michael pointed to the bottom section labeled *'Action Plan.'* "Finally, we move to **Commit**. This is where you map out clear, actionable steps. What must Lisa do, and what support will you provide?"

He filled in two boxes:

- Lisa: *'Attend leadership training.'*
- Manager: *'Assign stretch projects and provide feedback.'*

Sarah nodded slowly. "By the end of the conversation, we have a plan that we both own."

"Exactly," Michael said. "It's not just her career or your plan—it's a partnership."

Michael leaned back, gesturing to the completed Career Canvas. "Here's why this works: the 3C Framework provides the structure, and the Career Canvas offers the tool. Together, they help you move from understanding to action."

Sarah stared at the template, her mind racing. "It feels so... practical. Like I could use this tomorrow."

Michael smiled. "That's the idea. Co-creation isn't just a concept—it's a process. And the more you use it, the better you'll become at it.

Michael leaned back, watching Sarah absorb the information. If you're looking for a bit more inspiration, I'd recommend Bill Burnett's TEDx talk, "Designing Your Career." It's concise yet impactful, offering a valuable perspective on using design thinking to craft career paths.

Sarah smiled, tucking the sheet into her bag. "This feels manageable. Thanks, Michael."

LEVEL 10 LEADER

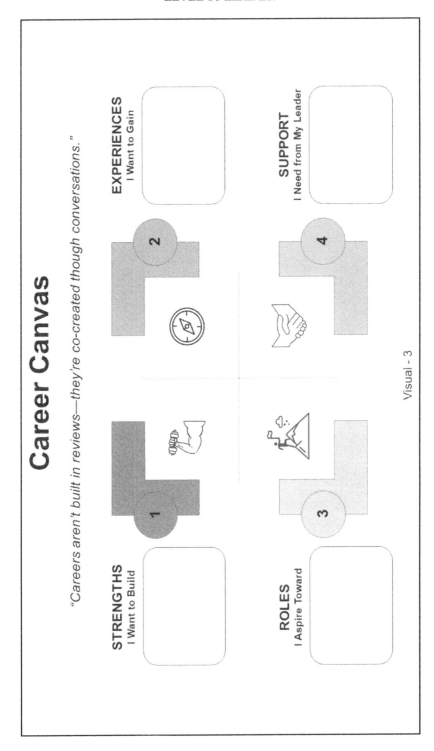

Visual - 3

Wednesday, April 16, 3:00 PM – Michael's Office, Crescent Tower, Midtown:

"Practice = Progress"

Sarah stepped into Michael's office, her nerves jangling like loose wires. With its bookshelves and framed photos of smiling teams, the room felt like a shrine to leadership success—starkly contrasting her self-doubt. At the center of the space was a round table with three chairs. A blank Career Canvas sat neatly in the middle, alongside a whiteboard and a marker.

Michael greeted her with his usual warmth. "Welcome, Sarah. Ready to dive in?"

"Define 'ready,'" Sarah quipped nervously, taking the chair opposite him.

Michael chuckled. "You'll do fine. Remember, this is about learning, not perfection."

The door opened, and a young man walked in, his relaxed smile easing some of Sarah's tension. "Hey, Sarah. I'm James."

"Hi," Sarah said, shaking his hand. "Thanks for helping with this."

James took his seat and glanced at the blank template. "I hear I'm the test subject," he said.

Michael grinned. "Exactly. Sarah's going to practice leading a career conversation with you. I'll step in if needed. Let's see where this goes."

Sarah took a deep breath and nodded. "Okay, here goes."

Sarah unfolded the Career Canvas and stared at the top section labeled *Aspirations*. She glanced at James. "So, uh… where do you see yourself in the next five years?"

James raised an eyebrow. "Five years? That's... a lot to think about. I'm not sure."

Michael interjected gently. "Let's ease into it, Sarah. Try asking something broader—make it conversational."

Sarah flushed but nodded. "Right. Okay, James, let's take a step back. What do you enjoy most about your current work?"

James leaned back, considering the question. "I like the problem-solving part—finding solutions and making things more efficient."

Sarah scribbled something on the canvas. "That's great. So, would you like to focus on building more technical expertise?"

James hesitated. "Maybe, but I've also been considering leadership roles. I'm not sure if I'm ready, though."

Michael leaned forward slightly. "Good insight, James. Sarah, what might you ask next to explore that hesitation?"

Sarah paused, then asked, "What about leadership that feels intimidating?"

James smiled faintly. "The responsibility, I guess. I worry about making mistakes that affect the whole team."

"That's totally valid," Sarah said, feeling a bit steadier now. "What about leadership excites you?"

"The chance to help others grow," James said after a moment. "And to have a bigger impact."

Sarah nodded, jotting down his responses under "Aspirations."

Moving to the next section, Sarah hesitated. "Okay, so... let's talk about opportunities. What do you think could help you build confidence in leadership?"

James shrugged. "I'm not sure. Perhaps consider shadowing someone or taking on a smaller leadership role?"

"That's a great start," Sarah said, glancing at Michael, who gave her an encouraging nod. "What if we also considered mentoring? It could allow you to guide others without the full responsibility of managing a team."

James tilted his head thoughtfully. "That sounds doable."

Michael chimed in. "Sarah, try framing this as a brainstorming session—make it collaborative."

Sarah brightened. "Right! James, what other ideas come to mind? Or is there something you've always wanted to try?"

James thought for a moment. "Well, I've always been curious about leading a project from start to finish. Maybe that's an option?"

Sarah smiled. "Absolutely. A small project could be a great way to test the waters."

Sarah shifted to the final section, *Action Plan*. "Okay, so... what are the next steps? I'll write down that you'll lead a project and... maybe look for a mentoring opportunity?"

Michael cleared his throat. "Sarah, remember that co-creation is a partnership. Don't assign—invite."

Sarah winced and turned back to James. "Right. What do you think would be a good next step?"

James considered. "I like the idea of leading a project. And mentoring sounds interesting, but I'd want to ease into it."

Sarah nodded. "That makes sense. How about we start with the project and revisit mentoring in a few months?"

"That works," James said, smiling.

Sarah jotted it down and added, "I'll check with the team to see if we can assign you a project soon. Does that sound good?"

"Definitely," James said.

Michael leaned back as the role-play came to an end. "Well done, Sarah. How do you feel?"

"A bit clumsy," Sarah admitted. "But better than when I started."

Michael smiled. "That's because you're learning. You asked thoughtful questions and adjusted as you went. Co-creation is about flexibility, and you showed that today."

James chimed in. "Honestly, Sarah, it felt natural. You were genuinely listening, and I appreciated that."

Michael added, "Here's the key takeaway: Co-creation isn't about perfection. It's about being present. You made mistakes, but you stayed engaged and brought the conversation back on track."

Sarah exhaled, a small smile spreading across her face. "Thanks. I feel like I can do this now."

Michael nodded. "That's the point of practice. Please apply what you've learned here and try it with someone on your team. Start small, and let the process evolve."

WIN WITH CAREERS

Tuesday, April 22, 11:00 AM – TechInnovate Headquarters

"Real Conversation, Real Growth"

Over the next few days, Sarah scheduled one-on-one career conversations with her team. Each meeting brought her closer to understanding their unique aspirations—and gave her small but meaningful wins.

Lisa's energy was unmistakable as she leaned forward, her eyes bright with enthusiasm. "I've always enjoyed working with different teams but never thought about leading a cross-functional project until now."

Sarah nodded, jotting notes on Lisa's Career Canvas. "That's a fantastic goal. What do you think would help you prepare for something like that?"

Lisa paused. "Maybe observing how those teams work together? I'd want to understand the dynamics before taking the lead."

"That's a smart approach," Sarah replied. "How about we start small? You could shadow one of the senior project leads during an upcoming initiative. Then we can identify a smaller project you could own."

Lisa's eyes lit up. "I love that idea. And maybe I could partner with Jane from Sales—she's amazing at bridging teams."

Sarah smiled. "Great suggestion. I'll reach out to Jane, and we'll set something up."

Lisa leaned back, visibly satisfied. "This is exciting. It's like I can actually see where I'm heading now."

LEVEL 10 LEADER

Mia walked in quietly, clutching her notebook, her posture slightly tense. As she sat down, Sarah gave a warm smile. "Thanks for taking the time, Mia. I've been really looking forward to hearing what's on your mind."

Mia took a breath. "I've always loved digging into problems and solving them quietly in the background... but lately, I've been wondering if I should push myself more—do something that stretches me."

Sarah leaned in. "That's such a valuable insight. What kind of stretch are you thinking?"

Mia hesitated. "I think... I'd like to work more directly with clients. Maybe support a client workshop or training. I want to see the real-world impact of what we build."

Sarah beamed. "That's an excellent fit for you. You have such a calm, thoughtful presence—I think clients would respond really well."

Mia smiled, a little surprised. "You really think so?"

"I do," Sarah said. Let's find a few upcoming sessions you can observe. Then, when you feel ready, we can consider co-facilitating a segment."

Mia's shoulders relaxed. "That sounds perfect. Thank you."

By the end of the week, Sarah flipped through the completed canvases with a mix of pride and reflection. The conversations with Lisa and Mia had been energizing. Still, they also reminded her that every person on the team had their own path.

She drew in a deep breath.

Next up: Karen and Tom.

And she was ready for it.

Thursday, April 24, 2:30 PM – Huddle Room, TechInnovate Headquarters

"One Inch at a Time"

Sarah sat in the small huddle room, the blank Career Canvas neatly laid out on the table. Her fingers fidgeted slightly as she glanced at the time. Tom was never late, but he wasn't exactly early either. Right on cue, the door creaked open, and Tom stepped in, his expression neutral but guarded.

"Hey, Tom," Sarah said with a warm smile. "Thanks for making time for this."

Tom nodded, pulling out a chair. "Sure. Let's see what this is about."

Sarah swallowed her nerves. *He's here. That's a start.* She gestured toward the canvas. I've been having these conversations with the team to understand everyone's goals better and how I can support them. I'd love to hear your thoughts."

Tom raised an eyebrow, crossing his arms. "Goals, huh? Not sure I have any groundbreaking ones."

"That's okay," Sarah said, keeping her tone light. "We don't have to focus on long-term plans. Let's start with what you enjoy most about your work."

Tom leaned back, considering the question. "I suppose I enjoy solving problems. The complex ones. That's what has kept me around for so long."

"That's a big strength," Sarah said, jotting it down under *Aspirations*. "What about the challenges? Are there areas where you feel stuck or could use more support?"

Tom hesitated. "Honestly? I don't feel stuck. But I do feel... underappreciated sometimes. It's as if the more complex problems I take on don't get noticed because they're behind the scenes."

Sarah nodded, sensing an opening. "That's important, Tom. Your work has a significant impact, even if it's not always immediately visible. What if we found ways to highlight your contributions more?"

Tom's skepticism softened slightly. "How would you do that?"

"Maybe we could create a knowledge-sharing session where you present some of the solutions you've developed," Sarah suggested. "It could help others learn from your expertise and give you the recognition you deserve."

Tom tilted his head. "That's... interesting. I never thought of it that way."

Encouraged by his response, Sarah leaned forward. "What about challenges you'd like to tackle next? If you could pick anything, what would it be?"

Tom rubbed his chin thoughtfully. "I've been eyeing that data optimization project. It's tricky, but it could make a big difference."

Sarah smiled. "That sounds like the perfect fit for your skills. How about we look into making that happen?"

Tom shrugged, but a flicker of interest appeared in his eyes. "Yeah, sure. Let's see."

As they wrapped up the conversation, Sarah summarized their discussion, filling out the *Opportunities* and *Action Plan* sections. "This was really helpful, Tom. Thanks for opening up."

Tom nodded, his expression still reserved but less guarded. "It was... different. In a good way."

As he exited the room, Sarah took a deep breath, a blend of relief and cautious optimism washing over her.

One inch at a time.

Karen entered the huddle room with her usual composed demeanor, arms crossed, as she sat across from Sarah. "All right," she said, her tone polite but distant. "What's this about?"

Sarah smiled, keeping her tone warm and friendly. "I've been having these conversations with the team to understand everyone's goals and how I can support them. Your perspective is critical to me, Karen."

Karen raised an eyebrow, her skepticism clear. "My perspective? You're the manager now. Isn't this more about you telling us what to do?"

Sarah exhaled slowly, steadying herself. "I don't see it that way. I believe the best results are achieved when we understand each other and work together. I'm here to listen first."

Karen leaned back slightly, her expression unreadable. "Okay. "What would you like to know?"

Sarah decided to tread carefully. "What do you enjoy most about your role? What keeps you motivated?"

Karen paused, her lips tightening as though weighing whether to answer. "I like seeing projects through—making sure everything stays on track. I'm good at making things run smoothly."

"That's a huge strength," Sarah said sincerely. "The team relies on your consistency and attention to detail. It's clear how much you contribute."

LEVEL 10 LEADER

Karen didn't respond, but her posture shifted slightly, signaling she was at least listening. Sarah pressed on gently. "Are there areas where you'd like to grow or explore more? Maybe things you've thought about but haven't had the chance to pursue?"

Karen hesitated before her voice hardened. "You mean like stepping into Mark's role? That's what I was aiming for—before you were brought in."

The room fell silent, Karen's words hanging like a challenge. Sarah's heart sank, but she kept her tone steady. "That's a critical point, Karen. And I understand why that would feel disappointing—maybe even unfair."

Karen crossed her arms tightly. "It's not just disappointing. It feels like none of my work was recognized. I've been here for years, doing everything right, and someone else gets the role."

Sarah nodded slowly, her voice calm but full of empathy. "Karen, I hear you. And I want to be honest with you—I didn't have any role in deciding my promotion. But I do have a role now. And I would love to play a big role in your next promotion."

Karen's posture shifted slightly, though her expression remained guarded. "What does that even mean?"

Sarah leaned forward. "It means I want to do everything I can to help you grow, build your skills, and get the recognition you deserve. I'd like to co-create a plan with you to make that happen."

Karen tilted her head, skepticism still evident. "Like what?"

"For starters," Sarah said, her tone measured, "we could work on building your visibility. Maybe Jessica could sponsor you for high-impact projects. We can also identify opportunities for you to take on leadership roles within the team, such as mentoring others or leading process improvements."

Karen's lips twitched into something resembling a smile. "Process improvements, huh? That's my kind of thing."

Sarah nodded eagerly. "Exactly. With Jessica's sponsorship, you'll gain the visibility you deserve while building your leadership profile. Would you be open to exploring that?"

Karen leaned back, considering. "I'd need to see how serious you are about this."

"That's fair," Sarah said, her voice steady. "How about we draft a plan together? We'll outline the steps, and I'll commit to supporting you in every way possible."

As their conversation drew to a close, Karen's posture softened even further. Sarah paused, looked Karen in the eye, and said, "Karen, I will be the second happiest person on this team the day you get promoted."

Karen blinked, momentarily taken aback. She didn't respond, but her expression softened—a flicker of something almost vulnerable crossing her face.

Karen stood, her tone still reserved but less rigid. "Thanks for this, Sarah. I'll admit—I wasn't expecting this kind of conversation."

"I'm glad we had it," Sarah said. Your growth is as essential to me as it is to anyone else on this team, and I'm committed to helping you achieve your goals."

Karen nodded again, this time with a faint but genuine smile. "We'll see how this goes."

As the door closed behind her, Sarah exhaled deeply, feeling both drained and hopeful. *It's a start. One inch at a time.*

LEVEL 10 LEADER

Friday, September 20, 12:30 PM – Corner Bistro, Downtown

"The Table Turns"

The team gathered around a large table near the office at a bustling lunch spot. The chatter of nearby diners and the clinking of plates created a lively backdrop as they took their seats. Lisa, as usual, took the lead in starting the conversation.

"So," Lisa said, leaning forward with a playful grin, "who else feels like they're working with a whole new version of Sarah lately?"

Mia smiled shyly. "I've noticed it too. She seems... more grounded. Like she's actually thinking about each of us—not just the work."

Tom raised an eyebrow as he sipped his coffee. "She's been doing these career conversations. Honestly, I expected something robotic. But... it wasn't. It felt real."

Lisa lit up. "Same. I felt seen. Like she cared about where I want to grow—not just what I can deliver next quarter."

Mia nodded. "When I told her I was interested in working with clients, she didn't just nod—she offered actual steps. She made it feel possible."

Tom leaned back, arms folded but face relaxed. "I'll admit it. After the town hall, I thought she was done. But that conversation with her? She didn't try to fix or defend. She just... listened."

Mia glanced at him, eyes wide. "Really?"

He smirked. "Yeah, don't get used to the praise. But she earned that one."

Lisa raised her glass of iced tea. "To progress, not perfection?"

Tom tapped his water bottle against hers. "Sure. That."

Karen, who had been quiet until now, finally spoke. "She and I had a tough one-on-one," she said, her voice softer than usual. "But... she didn't back away from it. She asked what I needed—not just what she expected."

Lisa leaned in, eyes sparkling. "What did you say?"

Karen half-smiled. "I asked for support getting visibility with leadership. She said she'd talk to Jessica about sponsorship. And... she followed through."

Tom looked impressed. "Now that's something."

Mia added quietly, "She really is trying."

Karen gave a slight nod. "Yeah. And I actually walked away feeling... heard. That's new."

As the conversation continued, the mood around the table grew lighter. They traded small stories of their one-on-ones with Sarah, each adding to a quiet sense of shared momentum.

"Remember when we thought she'd never recover after the town hall?" Lisa said, laughing softly.

Tom chuckled. "One step at a time."

Karen grinned. "One inch at a time."

The group burst into laughter, their camaraderie palpable. For the first time in weeks, it felt like they weren't just surviving—they were starting to move forward together.

LEVEL 10 LEADER

WIN WITH CAREERS

BEHAVIORS	ACCIDENTAL MANAGERS	LEVEL 10 LEADERS
What am I GETTING?	• Unclear growth paths • Talent stagnation or silent attrition • A team that feels stuck or unseen	• Energized team with clear direction • Career growth aligned with business needs • Increased loyalty, ownership, and aspiration
What am I DOING?	• Having career talks only during performance reviews • Making assumptions about what people want • Delegating career conversations to HR	• Holding regular career check-ins • Co-creating growth plans using the Career Canvas • Connecting roles to strengths, goals, and purpose
HOW am I SEEING?	• "Careers are personal—they'll figure it out." • "Growth means promotion." • "My job is to get results, not be a career coach."	• "Career growth is leadership in action." • "Development is about experiences, not just titles." • "Helping others grow is how I grow too."

The One Thing Challenge – Win with CAREERS

Choose one team member—and hold a 15-minute career conversation using the 3C Framework.

Ask these three questions:

1. **Connect:** What motivates you right now—beyond just your role?
2. **Collaborate:** What direction feels exciting or meaningful to you?
3. **Commit:** What's one small step we can take together in the next 30 days?

Take notes. Reflect. Follow up.

Careers aren't shaped by performance reviews.

They're shaped in conversations that say: *"I see you, and I'm with you."*

LEVEL 10 LEADER

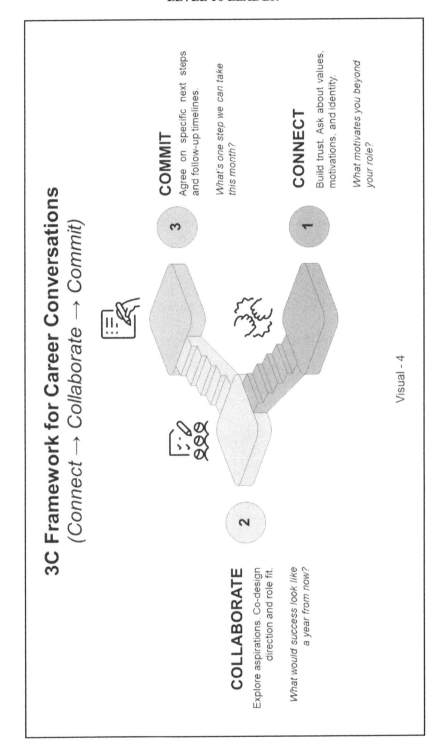

Visual - 4

Your Next Move

Was this chapter helpful?

If it sparked a new insight or gave you a practical tool, take 30 seconds to leave a quick review.

Your words might be the reason another leader takes the first step.

☞ Leave a review on Amazon

Ready to grow from a reader to a Level-10 Leader?

Unlock Level 10 Leadership Assessment, Workbook and more at resources.level10leader.com

References

1. Buckingham, Marcus, and Curt Coffman. *First, Break All the Rules: What the World's Greatest Managers Do Differently.* Simon & Schuster, 1999.

2. Goler, Lori, et al. *The Hard Truth About Soft Skills: Workplace Lessons Smart People Wish They'd Learned Sooner.* Harper Business, 2007.

3. Edmondson, Amy C. *The Fearless Organization: Creating Psychological Safety in the Workplace for Learning, Innovation, and Growth.* Wiley, 2018.

4. Kegan, Robert, and Lisa Laskow Lahey. *An Everyone Culture: Becoming a Deliberately Developmental Organization.* Harvard Business Review Press, 2016.

5. Gallup Research. *"How Managers Can Help Employees Thrive."* Gallup, 2020

PART-3

WINNING THE MIND

CHAPTER 5
Win With Goals

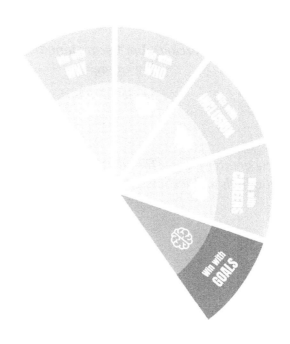

"Setting goals is the first step in turning the invisible into the visible."

— Tony Robbins

"If your dreams don't scare you, they're not big enough."

— Ellen Johnson Sirleaf

"The greater danger for most of us is not that our aim is too high and we miss it, but that it's too low and we reach it."

— Michelangelo

Saturday, May 3, 9:00 AM – Redwood Preserve Trailhead

"The Two Summits"

Sarah pulled into the parking lot of Redwood Preserve, a serene trailhead nestled in the hills. The early morning sun filtered through the towering trees, casting dappled light across the winding paths. She stepped out of her car, breathing in the crisp air, her thoughts still buzzing with her challenges as a team leader.

Michael stood near the trail map, hands in his pockets, looking at ease. "It's a perfect day for a hike," he said, greeting her warmly. Are you ready to stretch those legs and clear your mind?"

Sarah chuckled, adjusting her backpack. "I'm beginning to think your meeting spots are part of the lesson."

He grinned. "You're catching on. Come on, let's get started."

They began walking, the gravel crunching underfoot in a soothing rhythm. The scent of pine and earth filled the air, and birdsong created a calming backdrop. Michael handed Sarah a small trail guide with marked paths.

"This map shows the different routes we could take," Michael said, pointing to two summits marked on the map. "Summit One is a popular destination. It's a moderate climb, manageable for most hikers. Summit Two, on the other hand, is more challenging. It's steeper, less traveled, and will push you to your limits."

Sarah studied the map, her brow furrowing in concentration. "They both lead to amazing views. But Summit Two looks... intense."

LEVEL 10 LEADER

Michael nodded. "It is. But here's the question: Which summit do you think will grow the hiker more?"

Sarah hesitated, glancing at the trail map. "Probably the harder one. Even if you don't reach the top, the effort itself would teach you something."

Michael smiled. "Exactly. That's the power of a big, ambitious goal. It's not about guaranteeing success; it's about stretching beyond what you thought was possible. Now let me ask you this—if you put 80% effort into the harder trail, would it feel more rewarding than giving 100% on the easier one?"

Sarah thought for a moment. "I think it would. The harder trail might reveal things about myself I wouldn't discover otherwise."

Michael gestured toward the longer, winding path. "Let's take this trail today. It's not as steep as Summit Two, but it'll give us a glimpse of what it takes to keep going when the goal feels just out of reach."

As they walked, Michael pointed out the trail markers and resting points. "See those markers?" he asked, pausing by a post with an arrow. "They guide and remind us that we're on the right path. Without them, the journey would feel overwhelming."

"And the resting points?" Sarah asked, gesturing toward a bench overlooking a small creek.

"They're there to motivate us," Michael said. "To remind us why we're on this journey. In leadership, these are like the small wins that inspire your team."

As they approached a steep incline, Michael added, "Sometimes you must break the journey into smaller sections. Focus on one ridge at a time rather than the entire climb."

Sarah nodded, her steps purposeful as they tackled the incline. "It's about making the big goal feel manageable."

WIN WITH GOALS

Michael pointed to the distant summits as they reached the clearing, which offered a breathtaking view of the valley below. "That's the beauty of goals. They give us something to strive for, but the journey shapes us just as much as the destination."

Sarah leaned against a rock, her gaze fixed on the distant peaks. "I feel like I'm starting to understand, but there's still so much to learn."

Michael turned to her, his tone shifting to one of reflection. "Let me ask you something. If this had been our first meeting—if I had invited you to tackle this trail right after your promotion—how would it have gone?"

Sarah chuckled nervously. "Honestly? I probably would've felt overwhelmed. I was barely keeping my head above water back then."

Michael nodded. "Exactly. Winning with goals isn't about jumping straight into ambition. It's about timing. Remember where you started—discovering your 'Why,' building trust with your team, fostering inclusion. Without those foundational wins, setting ambitious goals would have felt forced, maybe even demoralizing."

"So, you're saying I needed to win the spirit and the heart first?" Sarah asked.

Michael smiled. "Yes. Purpose and connection come first. They ground you and give you clarity and trust—both in yourself and your team. Only then can you begin discussing the goals that stretch potential and drive progress."

Sarah's expression softened, her earlier nervousness replaced with a sense of realization. "It makes sense. I wouldn't have been ready for this conversation before. Now, I feel like I can see how everything fits together."

Michael gestured toward the summits. "That's why the timing of leadership conversations is crucial. A great goal at the wrong time can feel like a burden. But at the right time? It becomes a challenge worth embracing."

They sat on a wooden bench at the overlook, the valley stretching out in shades of green and gold. Neither spoke for a while, simply taking in the view.

Michael finally broke the silence. "Sarah, today wasn't just about the hike. Reflect on what you experienced—the markers, the resting points, and the choices along the way. Each of those elements mirrors how we set and achieve goals."

Sarah tilted her head, her curiosity piqued. "You mean, like how goals should guide us but also inspire us?"

Michael smiled. "Exactly. But here's the thing—I want you to reflect on what this journey taught you about goal setting. Take a few days to think about it. Write down your thoughts, and let's meet again to discuss."

Sarah nodded, a spark of excitement flickering in her eyes. "I will. This... this makes sense in a way I didn't expect."

Michael stood, gesturing toward the trailhead. "Good. Great leadership isn't about giving people answers but helping them find their own."

As they returned down the trail, Sarah's mind raced with questions and insights. She felt the stirrings of clarity as if the path ahead was finally coming into focus.

SMART Goal Builder

"A clear goal doesn't just guide action—it builds belief."

SMART Element	Definition	Example "I" Statement
S – Specific	The goal is focused, clear, and unambiguous.	"I know exactly what I need to accomplish."
M – Measurable	Tracks progress using quantifiable metrics.	"I will boost our email response rate by 20% over the next quarter."
A – Achievable	Sets a realistic target within available resources and constraints.	"I will schedule 3 client meetings per week, based on current lead volume."
R – Relevant	Aligns with company goals and business priorities.	"I will improve customer satisfaction scores to support our service excellence initiative."
T – Time-bound	Includes a specific deadline or timeframe.	"I will complete the competitor analysis report by June 15th."

Adapted from the original SMART Goals framework introduced by George T. Doran (1981)

Visual - 5

LEVEL 10 LEADER

Thursday, May 8, 9:00 AM – Conference Room, TechInnovate Headquarters:

"The BHAG Begins"

The conference room hummed quietly as the team settled into their seats. Sunlight streamed through the large windows, illuminating the whiteboard at the front, where Sarah had written a single phrase:

"Building the Future Together."

Unlike past meetings, there were no slides or rigid agendas. Sarah stood to the side, holding a marker—ready to facilitate, not dictate.

"Thanks for coming," Sarah began, her tone open and conversational. "Today isn't about me telling you what we need to achieve. It's about deciding together what we want to build—as a team and as individuals."

Lisa leaned forward, intrigued. "So... where do we start?"

Sarah smiled. "That's up to you. What should this team focus on to succeed this quarter?"

The room was quiet for a beat. Then Tom spoke, his voice steady. "Client response times. That's been a thorn in our side for months."

Lisa nodded. "That's Valid. But if we don't deliver the upcoming feature update, that's going to cost us trust and reputation."

Karen crossed her arms. "They're both important. But neither will hold if our internal systems stay broken. The real issue is the underlying process delays."

Mia added quietly, "And those delays aren't just operational—they hurt client trust. People are waiting too long to hear back."

The discussion came alive. Lisa argued that quick wins with clients mattered more. Karen countered that patchwork wouldn't fix a failing system. Tom pushed for balance. Mia offered that a shared goal might help unify all the concerns.

Sarah raised a hand gently. "These are all great perspectives. Let me introduce a question I recently came across in *The ONE Thing* by Keller and Papasan:

'What's the ONE thing we can do, such that by doing it, everything else becomes easier or unnecessary?'"

The room stilled.

Tom leaned forward. "If we fix response times, we ease client tension, reduce internal stress, and maybe even improve rollout communication."

Lisa nodded. "It's the gateway problem. Solve that, and everything else becomes smoother."

Karen added, "It'll also force us to look at broken processes. It's like pressure testing the system."

Mia said softly, "And for clients, it shows we care. It would change how they feel about working with us."

Sarah nodded, then posed another question. "What would this look like if we stretched ourselves—made it bold?"

Karen arched an eyebrow. "You mean, like, under-an-hour response times?"

Lisa's eyes widened. "What if we actually made that the goal?"

Tom let out a low whistle. "That's a moonshot. We're not even consistent with 12-hour turnarounds."

"It's a BHAG," Lisa replied, smiling. "It's not meant to feel safe."

Karen leaned in slightly. "It'd mean rebuilding a lot. But it could be worth it."

Mia added, "Imagine how that would feel—for us and the client. Fast, responsive, human."

Sarah gave the group a moment to sit with the idea. Then she asked, "What's the worst that happens if we fall short?"

Tom shrugged. "We still drastically improve."

"And the best?" Sarah prompted.

Lisa's voice lit up. "We redefine ourselves."

Karen smiled faintly. "We prove we're more than just capable—we're high-impact."

Sarah turned to the board and wrote:

Achieve sub-hour client response times by year-end.

"This is our Big, Hairy, Audacious Goal. Even if we don't hit it 100%, imagine how far we'll go."

They began breaking it down into SMART terms:

- **Specific:** Client response times. Clear and measurable.
- **Measurable:** Weekly CRM dashboards. Real-time visibility.
- **Achievable:** Tough but possible with automation and rethinking processes.
- **Relevant:** It directly affects trust, satisfaction, and internal clarity.

- **Time-bound:** Twelve months.

They paused. Sarah looked around. "What does this goal mean—to you?"

Karen spoke first. "For clients, it builds trust. For us, it builds credibility."

Lisa added, "It elevates our reputation. It's a leadership moment."

Tom nodded. "It'd reduce firefighting. It'd make work less reactive."

Mia smiled. "And it would make me proud to say, 'We did that.'"

Sarah underlined the final goal:

"Achieve sub-hour client response times by year-end—transforming client experience, team efficiency, and how we see ourselves."

The room fell into thoughtful silence. Sarah looked at them and said, "Let's take the rest of the day to reflect. Tomorrow, we'll start mapping the how."

As they exited, the energy had shifted. The hallway was quiet, but their steps felt more confident.

Lisa glanced at Karen. "Okay, I'll admit it—that was bold. But... it's starting to feel doable."

Karen smirked. "Doable... maybe. But only because she made us believe it was."

Tom added, "She's different now. Feels like she's with us—not above us."

Mia nodded. "For the first time, it feels like our goal—not just her ask."

Karen tilted her head. "Did you notice she didn't push back on the resistance? She let us get there ourselves."

Tom chuckled. "She's earning it."

Lisa grinned. "She's trying. And I think... it's starting to work."

Friday, May 9, 10:00 AM – Conference Room, TechInnovate Headquarters

"The Roadmap and The Role"

The following day, the team gathered again in the same conference room. Tom's tray of coffees sat in the middle of the table, already half-empty. On the whiteboard, yesterday's bold commitment still stood, daring them to figure out how to make it happen:

"Reduce first response times to under an hour by year-end."

Sarah took her seat among the group, letting the room settle. "Good morning. How does everyone feel about the goal we set yesterday?"

Karen glanced at the board, arms crossed. "It's still huge. But... I'm starting to think it's possible."

Lisa nodded. "If we break it down quarter by quarter, it doesn't feel so overwhelming."

Tom grumbled, though with a smirk. "Still terrifying. But yeah—let's figure it out."

Mia added softly, "It's ambitious, but it matters. And we'll be proud of how we worked together—not just the result."

Sarah smiled. "That's exactly what we're here to do. Let's build the roadmap."

Lisa tapped her pen thoughtfully. "If we're going to consistently hit under an hour in Q4, what needs to happen in Q3?"

Karen leaned forward. "By then, everyone needs to be trained on the new workflows and tools. There should be no gaps, no delays."

Tom added, "Which means Q2 is all about testing those workflows—stress-testing them, automating what we can, and finding out where they break."

Mia suggested, "We could also map the client journey. Talk to some of the more frustrated clients and see what patterns emerge. That might show us what really needs fixing."

Lisa nodded. "And that puts Q1 squarely in discovery mode—diagnosing problems, mapping bottlenecks, and collecting data."

Sarah stood and drew a timeline on the board—Q4, Q3, Q2, Q1—marking their milestones as the team spoke. The energy sharpened as they worked backward from bold to practical.

Karen pointed at the Q1 milestone: *Identify bottlenecks and root causes.*

"If that's where we need to land by March, what's doable in January?"

Lisa offered, "Start by analyzing CRM data to pinpoint the most frequent delays."

LEVEL 10 LEADER

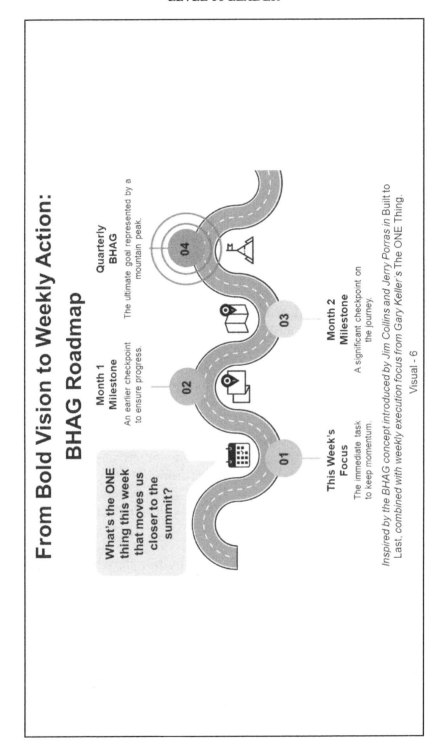

Tom nodded. "And gather feedback from the frontline folks. They know exactly what slows them down."

Karen added, "We can also tag cases with reasons for delay—'waiting on approval,' 'unclear client input,' that sort of thing. We'll get clarity on where the friction is."

Mia leaned in. "What about mapping emotional spikes, too—moments when clients get frustrated or when team stress peaks? That might show us pressure points we wouldn't catch in data alone."

Lisa smiled. "By the end of January, we'll have a real picture of what's broken."

Sarah broke January into four weeks on the board. "Great start. What's Week 1?"

Karen replied, "Start pulling and sorting the data. Keep it simple. Just get the raw insights."

Tom added, "We can divide the work—each of us takes a chunk to review, and then we can share the takeaways."

Sarah nodded. "You're building a strong foundation. Let's keep going."

As the roadmap filled the board, Sarah turned back to the group. "One more piece—accountability. How do we ensure we follow through?"

Lisa spoke first. "Accountability partners. Pair up and check in weekly. It keeps things grounded and human."

Karen agreed. "And pair people with different strengths. Someone focused on details with someone who thinks big."

Tom raised a finger. "Let's not forget encouragement. This won't be easy. We need to support each other, not just check boxes."

Mia added, "We could even rotate partners halfway through. It keeps perspectives fresh."

Lisa nodded. "And keep check-ins short—fifteen minutes a week. Enough to stay focused without feeling like another meeting."

Sarah captured their input:

Individual Accountability

- Pair up with accountability partners
- Weekly 15-minute check-ins: progress, challenges, next steps
- Strategic pairings based on complementary strengths
- Optional mid-point partner switch for new perspectives

"Let's talk pairings," Sarah said. "Any preferences?"

Lisa and Karen exchanged a knowing glance. "We'll team up," Lisa said.

Tom looked across at Mia. "Want to team up?"

Mia smiled. "Sure."

Tom smirked, glancing at Sarah. "Looks like you're stuck with the boss."

Sarah laughed. "I've had worse luck."

Lisa paused. "Could we bring in someone outside the team to keep us accountable, too? Someone neutral but firm?"

Tom raised an eyebrow. "Like who? Another team lead?"

Karen tilted her head. "What about Jessica? She's already invested in us. She'd push us—and she wouldn't let us off easy."

The room went quiet as they considered it.

WIN WITH GOALS

Mia spoke gently. "She'd hold a high bar. And it would mean we're serious."

Tom nodded. "She's fair. Tough, but fair."

Lisa added, "It would raise our visibility too. It shows we're not hiding—we're proud of this goal."

Sarah nodded. "I agree. This is a goal worth being held accountable for. And Jessica's the right person."

Karen raised an eyebrow. "Okay, but who will lead the updates with her?"

Sarah turned to her, her tone confident. "You, Karen. You've got the voice, the credibility, and the insight. And I believe you're ready."

Karen blinked. "Me?"

Lisa beamed. "You'd be perfect. Seriously."

Tom shrugged. "Better you than me. But yeah, you've got the respect."

Mia nodded. "And the presence. She'll listen to you."

Karen stood a little straighter. "Alright. I'll do it."

As the team gathered their things, the room felt lighter. The once-daunting BHAG now felt real—and within reach.

Tom and Lisa traded light-hearted jabs as they left. Mia and Karen lingered, quietly reviewing the next steps.

Karen remained by the whiteboard, tracing the roadmap with her eyes. When the room had cleared, she turned to Sarah.

"Hey," she said softly. "Thanks. For trusting me. And for keeping your word."

LEVEL 10 LEADER

Sarah looked up. "My word?"

Karen smiled. "You said you'd back my growth. You're doing more than that."

Sarah's voice was warm. "You're not being given anything, Karen. You're claiming what you've earned."

Karen's expression shifted, touched. "Still—thank you. This team... it's different. And I think it's because of you."

Sarah smiled back. "And I'm different because of all of you. We're building something new—together."

Karen nodded. "That's the part that matters."

As Karen left, Sarah stood alone, her eyes returning to the whiteboard. It wasn't just a plan—it was a symbol of what was now possible.

This is what co-creation looks like, she thought. *One step at a time. One person at a time.*

WIN WITH GOALS

BEHAVIORS	ACCIDENTAL MANAGERS	LEVEL 10 LEADERS
What am I GETTING?	• Conflicting priorities • Missed deadlines or scattered focus • A team unclear about what matters most	• Aligned priorities and shared ownership • Focused energy on high-impact outcomes • A motivated team pulling in the same direction
What am I DOING?	• Setting vague or shifting targets • Pushing tasks instead of rallying around outcomes • Measuring success reactively	• Co-creating SMART goals. • Linking goals to the team's WHY and strengths • Tracking and celebrating progress consistently
HOW am I SEEING?	• "Goals are about hitting numbers." • "People need to be told what to do." • "Setting stretch goals leads to burnout."	• "Goals bring focus and purpose." • "People commit more when they help shape the goal." • "Clarity creates momentum - one step at a time."

The One Thing Challenge:

Challenge your team to define ONE bold, shared goal and build it together using SMART, BHAG, and accountability.

1. **Start with a bold question:**

   "If we could accomplish ONE bold thing this quarter that would make us proud—and raise the bar—what would it be?"

2. **Shape it using SMART:**

   Ensure the goal is:

   Specific • Measurable • Achievable • Relevant • Timebound

3. **Assign shared ownership:**

   Pair team members to co-lead this goal. Set up a **15-minute weekly rhythm** to review progress and unblock issues together.

   Big goals don't scare high-trust teams. They stretch them—and bond them.

   Set one bold goal. Make it SMART. Track it together.

Your Next Move

Was this chapter helpful?

If it sparked a new insight or gave you a practical tool, take 30 seconds to leave a quick review.

Your words might be the reason another leader takes the first step.

☞ Leave a review on Amazon

Ready to grow from a reader to a Level-10 Leader?

Unlock Level 10 Leadership Assessment, Workbook and more at resources.level10leader.com

References

1. Collins, Jim. Good to Great: Why Some Companies Make the Leap... and Others Don't. Harper Business, 2001.

2. Keller, Gary, and Jay Papasan. The ONE Thing: The Surprisingly Simple Truth Behind Extraordinary Results. Bard Press, 2013.

3. Gallup Research. "Why Accountability Improves Team Performance." Gallup, 2020.

4. Dweck, Carol S. Mindset: The New Psychology of Success. Ballantine Books, 2007.

5. Edmondson, Amy C. The Fearless Organization: Creating Psychological Safety in the Workplace for Learning, Innovation, and Growth. Wiley, 2018.

CHAPTER 6
Win With Growth

"Tell me, and I forget. Teach me, and I remember. Involve me, and I learn."

— Benjamin Franklin

"The only thing worse than training your employees and having them leave is not training them and having them stay."

— Henry Ford

"Train people well enough so they can leave, treat them well enough so they don't want to."

— Richard Branson

Tuesday, May 27, 6:30 PM – Local Community Basketball Court

"PRACTICE, PIVOT, PERSIST"

As Sarah stepped into the local basketball court, the sharp squeak of sneakers against polished wood filled the air. The players were mid-drill, weaving through cones, passing, and pivoting with quick, practiced movements. A coach blew his whistle, pausing to correct a player's stance.

Michael greeted her at the entrance with a warm smile. "Welcome to one of my favorite classrooms," he said.

Sarah raised an eyebrow, glancing around the bustling court. "A basketball court?"

Michael chuckled. "Why not? Learning happens everywhere, Sarah. Come on, let's watch."

They settled onto the bleachers as the players transitioned into a free-throw drill. The coach walked along the line, offering pointers to some and encouraging others. One player seemed particularly frustrated, missing shot after shot.

Sarah winced as the ball bounced off the rim again. "Poor kid."

"Keep watching," Michael said.

The player took a deep breath, adjusted their stance slightly, and released the ball. It swished cleanly through the hoop. They smiled, energized, and repeated the motion, sinking two more in a row.

Michael gestured toward the court. "You just saw the 10-20-70 model in action."

LEVEL 10 LEADER

Sarah tilted her head. "I'm not familiar with that."

"It's a framework for adult learning," Michael explained. "Approximately 10% of learning comes from structured instruction, such as when a coach demonstrates techniques. Another 20% comes from social learning—watching teammates and getting feedback. But the majority—70%—comes from doing. Experiment, practice, and fail until you figure it out."

Sarah nodded slowly, her gaze fixed on the players. "That makes sense. The player who kept missing—he didn't give up. He adjusted until he got it right."

Michael smiled. "Exactly. Growth doesn't happen from sitting back and watching. It happens when you step into the arena, take risks, and learn from what doesn't work."

The 10-20-70 Rule for Real Growth

- **LEARNING**
  (books, webinars, courses)
- **OBSERVING**
  (feedback, mentoring, peer learning)
- **DOING**
  (real work, stretch projects, reflection-in-action)

10%
20%
70%

> Growth doesn't happen by learning alone—it happens by doing, with support and intention

Inspired by the 70-20-10 Learning Model developed by Michael M. Lombardo and Robert W. Eichinger at the Center for Creative Leadership, emphasizing learning through doing, coaching, and formal instruction.

Visual - 7

The players switched to a scrimmage. A young player tried a daring pass only to have it intercepted. Their teammates groaned, and the coach blew the whistle, pulling them aside. After a quick conversation, the player tried again, this time successfully threading the ball through the defense.

Sarah leaned forward. "They're learning by doing—and not being afraid to fail."

Michael nodded. "That's the essence of a growth mindset. It's about embracing effort, viewing mistakes as opportunities, and seeking feedback to improve."

"Easier said than done," Sarah murmured. "Failure can feel... discouraging."

Michael turned to her, his expression thoughtful. "That's true, but think about this: What happens when a leader fears failure? What kind of culture does that create?"

Sarah frowned, the question sinking in. "A culture where people play it safe. Where they're afraid to take risks or try new things."

Michael pointed toward the court. "Exactly. However, when leaders model resilience and frame failure as a stepping stone, they unlock potential—not just in themselves, but in their teams."

The coach clapped his hands, gathering the players into a huddle. He asked each to share one personal goal for the session. Sarah noticed their engagement as the players voiced their targets—improving free throws, better defending, and increasing speed.

Michael gestured toward the group. "That's personal accountability. They set their own goals and take ownership of their progress. It's not about the coach pushing them—it's about them pushing themselves."

WIN WITH GROWTH

Sarah crossed her arms, her brow furrowed. "How do I encourage that in my team? How do I make them feel accountable for their growth?"

Michael smiled. "Start by modeling it yourself. Show them what it looks like to embrace learning, seek feedback, and persist through challenges. Then, create an environment where they feel safe doing the same."

Michael stood as the scrimmage ended, motioning for Sarah to follow. "Here's your challenge," he said. "Consider integrating the 10-20-70 model into your team's growth strategy: structured learning, social collaboration, and hands-on experience."

He reached into his bag, pulling out a copy of *Mindset* by Carol Dweck. "This will help you dive deeper into the growth mindset. Read it, then reflect: How can you personally model and promote this mindset for your team?"

Sarah took the book, flipping through the pages. "This feels like a lot to take in."

Michael smiled. "Growth always does at first. But remember, it's not about being perfect—it's about showing up, trying, and learning along the way."

As Sarah walked out of the gym, the sounds of basketballs still echoing behind her, she couldn't help but feel inspired. The lessons of persistence, learning, and accountability were already taking root.

LEVEL 10 LEADER

Thursday, May 15, 10:00 AM – Jessica's Office, TechInnovate Headquarters

"The Impossible Deadline"

The team settled into their seats in Jessica's office, their expressions a mix of confidence and apprehension. The room was bright but tense, the silence broken only by the quiet click of Karen's pen. She clutched a folder of progress reports and glanced at Sarah for reassurance before beginning.

"Thank you for having us, Jessica," Karen began, her voice steady. "We're pleased to report a 15% reduction in client response times in Q1 and a clear roadmap for the next three quarters to hit our year-end BHAG."

Jessica nodded as Karen outlined key milestones. Lisa highlighted operational wins and the successful rollout of new client communication tools. Tom added insights about backend restructuring and shared recent metrics. Mia contributed a soft but impactful point about the shift in client sentiment captured through early feedback loops.

When they finished, Jessica leaned forward, her gaze locked on the team. "I appreciate the progress—it's clear you've all put in a meaningful effort. But I want to challenge you."

The room went still.

Jessica continued, her voice calm but resolute. "The company is at an inflection point. Reducing response times isn't just a goal—it's a competitive advantage we need now. That's why I want you to achieve your BHAG in six months, not twelve."

The silence that followed was instant—and heavy.

Tom's eyes widened. "Six months? That's half the time we scoped."

WIN WITH GROWTH

Lisa frowned, flipping through her notes. "We've only just started scaling the bigger changes. That pace would be intense."

Karen leaned forward. "It's not impossible... but it would mean restructuring everything. Every quarter plan. Every assumption."

Mia, composed, spoke next. "We'd need to eliminate anything that doesn't move the needle. It's not just about doing more—it's about doing less, better."

Jessica met their eyes. "I know it's ambitious. But I also know you're not the same team you were months ago. You've evolved. This is your chance to lead from the front—and redefine what's possible."

Karen turned to Sarah, her voice quieter now. "What do you think? Can we even do this?"

Sarah took a deep breath, feeling the weight of everyone's eyes—and the challenge ahead. "Jessica," she said calmly, "we're committed. But the acceleration is daunting. We'll need a few days to reassess and plan."

Jessica's expression softened. "Of course. I'm not asking for miracles—I'm asking for bold thinking. Regroup, and when you return, I want to hear how you'll make this real."

The team stepped into the hallway, tension trailing behind them like a shadow. For several steps, no one spoke—until Tom broke the silence.

"Six months. She's not playing."

Lisa flipped back through her notebook. "No. But she's right. If we hit this, it changes everything—for us, for the company."

Karen exhaled slowly. "It won't be about tweaking timelines anymore. We'll need a total redesign—how we prioritize, how we deliver, how we communicate."

Mia added gently, "We'll have to stay tightly aligned. The pace will challenge us, but so will the pressure. We'll burn out fast if we lose sight of the *why*."

Sarah paused in the middle of the hallway and turned to face them. "I know it's overwhelming. Honestly, it should be. But we've come so far already. Let's take the weekend, reflect, and regroup on Monday. One layer at a time—we'll figure it out."

The team nodded—not yet fully confident but unafraid to begin.

That night, Sarah sat at her desk, notes from the day sprawled out before her. The line from Jessica echoed in her head:

"I'm not asking for miracles—I'm asking for bold thinking."

She opened her journal and wrote across a fresh page:

How do we make the impossible possible—together?

She underlined the word **together**, then closed the journal and exhaled.

This was the growth mindset, alive.

And tomorrow, she would lead with it.

Monday, May 19, 2:00 PM – Huddle Room, TechInnovate Headquarters:

"The Lens That Changes Everything"

The air in the huddle room felt dense with quiet tension. Coffee cups sat untouched. Sarah stood by the whiteboard, marker in hand, but hadn't written a word. The pressure of the six-month BHAG hung in the air like fog.

She took a slow breath. "I know this feels like a lot. Overwhelming, even. Maybe... impossible."

Tom gave a dry laugh. "Impossible might be generous."

Lisa nodded, arms crossed. "It's not that we're not all in. But we were already at capacity. Now the timeline's slashed in half?"

Karen looked at Sarah, her voice quiet. "Honestly? I'm not even sure where we start."

Sarah nodded, letting the silence stretch instead of rushing to fill it. Then, gently: "I hear you. All of you. But what if... we pressed pause on the *how* for a moment?"

She turned to the whiteboard and raised her marker. "What if we looked at this goal differently?"

"What if this BHAG isn't just something we're supposed to achieve," she said slowly, "but something we're meant to grow into?"

The room quieted. Something about that phrasing landed.

Karen tilted her head. "So... you're saying the real purpose isn't the number?"

"Exactly," Sarah replied. "The outcome matters, but the real win is becoming the kind of team that makes goals like this—and harder ones—inevitable."

Tom raised an eyebrow. "So the point of the BHAG... is *us*?"

"Yes," Sarah said, a small smile forming. "The journey shapes us. Success isn't just about hitting metrics—it's about who we become in the process."

She returned to the whiteboard and drew three interlocking circles: **See ➔ Do ➔ Get**.

SEE → DO → GET: The Growth Mindset Loop

SEE
What I believe about myself, others, or the situation

DO
The actions I take based on what I see

GET
The results I create, which reinforce how I see things

Inspired by the SEE-DO-GET model popularized by Stephen R. Covey and FranklinCovey, illustrating the reinforcing loop between mindset, behavior, and outcomes.

Visual - 8

"This is something I learned from Michael," she labeled each circle. "It's called the See–Do–Get a cycle."

She pointed to the first. "How we *see* the challenge shapes what we *do*. And what we do determines what we *get*—our results."

Mia leaned forward slightly. "So if we're not getting what we want... it's because we're seeing it through the wrong lens?"

"Exactly," Sarah nodded. "We usually rush into doing. But lasting change starts upstream—with perspective."

Tom crossed his arms. "So if we keep seeing this as an impossible deadline, of course, we're going to hesitate, stall, play it safe."

Lisa chimed in, "But if we see it as growth? Or transformation? Then we act bolder, more creatively, and faster."

Sarah smiled. "That shift—that's where breakthrough begins."

She returned to the board and wrote two words beneath the circles: **Growth Mindset**.

"This is the most important lens we can adopt. A growth mindset means seeing challenges as catalysts for development. It's believing that effort leads to mastery—and that failure isn't fatal."

Karen frowned. "So... it's okay to fail now?"

Sarah chuckled softly. "Failure forward is okay. It's what we *do* with failure that counts."

Tom leaned back. "So if we mess up on the way... it's not the end?"

"No," Sarah said firmly. "It's feedback. It's part of the transformation. And I believe if we focus on who we're becoming, we'll unlock new ways to succeed."

Mia spoke up, voice gentle but precise. "That actually feels… freeing. Like we don't have to know everything yet. We just have to grow—fast—together."

Lisa added, "We're used to delivering results. Maybe it's time we start delivering growth."

Sarah capped her marker and stepped back. "I want to leave you with something to think about today."

She turned and underlined the words she wrote:

The real purpose of a goal isn't just to achieve it—it's to become the kind of team that can.

She looked around. No one was scrolling. No one was watching the clock.

"Take the rest of the afternoon. Reflect. Journal. Talk to each other. Ask yourself:

- Who do we need to become to make this goal inevitable?
- And what do we need to *see differently* to start that transformation today?

Let's come back tomorrow and share what comes up."

As the team filed out, the energy had shifted. The fear hadn't disappeared—but it had shape now. The unknown had been renamed: **growth**.

Sarah stayed behind, slowly erasing the board. But in the bottom corner, she wrote softly to herself:

Transformation starts with how we see.

She paused, then added:

And we're starting to see it—together.

Tuesday, May 20, 10:00 AM – Huddle Room, TechInnovate Headquarters

"Bold Thinking, Bold Moves"

The huddle room buzzed with quiet energy. Yesterday's reframing had shifted the mood from doubt to determination—but Sarah knew clarity wouldn't come without digging deeper. She stood at the whiteboard, marker in hand, as the team settled in.

"Yesterday," Sarah began, "we agreed that success isn't just about hitting the goal—it's about becoming the kind of team that can. Today, we're going to explore what that takes—not by working harder but by thinking differently."

Tom crossed his arms, tone dry. "So... this is the part where we blow things up?"

Sarah smiled. "If by 'blow things up' you mean challenge our old assumptions—yes. We're using the *See–Do–Get* framework. Let's figure out what's kept us stuck—and what will set us free."

She drew a large circle on the board and labeled it **SEE**.

"Let's start here. What are we currently *seeing*—about the goal, the timeline, or ourselves—that might be holding us back?"

Lisa raised her hand first. "We're assuming this fits into our old workflows. But those were designed for steady improvement—not a six-month moonshot."

Karen added, "We're also seeing this as our siloed responsibility. But unless product, support, and marketing align around it, we're pushing a boulder uphill."

Tom nodded. "We still treat Jessica like an evaluator, not a collaborator. If this is *her* top priority, we need her as an ally."

Mia, thoughtful, added, "And we're seeing failure as something to avoid. But if we're trying to innovate, we should expect some missteps."

Karen glanced around the room. "One more thing—we keep seeing ourselves as executors. But if we're going to hit a BHAG in six months, we have to start seeing ourselves as *builders*. Maybe even visionaries."

Sarah nodded as she filled the board. "These are strong insights. Let's keep going."

She drew a second circle labeled **DO**.

"If we shift the way we see—what needs to change in what we *do*?"

Lisa leaned in. "We stop assuming the old way works. We question everything—even the sacred cows."

Tom added, "More action, less approval-seeking. If we trust each other, we move faster."

Mia said, "We declutter. Cut meetings, reports—anything that doesn't serve the BHAG."

Karen spoke slowly. "We decentralize. Give micro-teams authority to solve problems in real-time."

Lisa tapped her pen. "And we propose a sprint week—a hackathon across teams focused entirely on this goal."

Tom chuckled. "And we kill anything that starts with, 'Well, that's how we've always done it.'"

The group laughed—but the truth of it stuck.

Sarah drew the final circle: **GET**.

"If we change what we see and do—what do we *get*?"

Tom was quick. "Respect. Not just internally—industry-wide."

Lisa nodded. "And pride. We'll prove that big goals can be real when culture supports them."

Karen leaned forward. "We won't just meet a target. We'll shift how this organization thinks about speed and possibility."

Mia's voice was soft but clear. "We become the kind of team people *want* to work with."

Sarah paused, letting that land. "Exactly. So… let's define what bold action looks like right now."

She underlined the word **BOLD** on the whiteboard.

Tom leaned forward. "Ask Jessica to make this the #1 company priority. Publicly. No competing KPIs."

Lisa added, "And propose a full sprint week—one that pulls in cross-functional teams and eliminates distractions."

Karen added, "Request what we need—AI tools, automation, even short-term contractors."

Mia said, "And if we fail, we recover fast. That mindset has to be built into the plan."

Sarah nodded. "Let's structure this."

She drew three columns on the board: **Start. Stop. Continue.**

Together, they filled it out:

- **Start:** Sprint week, cross-functional tiger teams, AI and automation pilots, bold resource asks.
- **Stop:** Waiting for approvals, legacy workflows, low-impact metrics.
- **Continue:** Weekly check-ins, peer accountability, transparent wins and lessons.

Karen studied the board. "If we pitch this to Jessica, we need it bulletproof."

Sarah nodded. "Then we divide and conquer. Each of us owns one part of the proposal. Anticipate objections. Bring solutions."

Lisa raised an eyebrow. "Do you think she'll say yes?"

Sarah smiled. "We won't know unless we bring her something *worth* saying yes to."

As the team gathered their things, quiet conversations filled the hallway.

Mia glanced over. "This could change how teams work here—for good."

Lisa nodded. "If it works, it won't just reset our bar. It'll reset the culture."

Karen lingered by the board, scanning their notes. "If Jessica backs us... this becomes the future of how things get done."

Sarah looked over. "And if she doesn't?"

Karen smirked. "Then we prove her wrong—with results."

Sarah chuckled. "Now *that's* a growth mindset."

Friday, May 23, 3:00 PM – Jessica's Office, TechInnovate Headquarters

"The Pitch That Landed"

Jessica's office was sleek and expansive, with floor-to-ceiling windows framing the skyline. But the room's attention was squarely focused on Sarah's bold proposal.

Jessica sat at the head of the table, skimming the document with a practiced eye. Her expression was unreadable, save for the slight arch of one eyebrow. Sarah stood off to the side, giving her team the floor.

"Well," Jessica began, her voice measured. "This is... ambitious. You're asking for cross-departmental alignment, a sprint week, additional resources, and a reprioritization of company metrics. That's a major pivot."

Karen leaned forward, steady and poised. "Because the goal demands a major pivot. If we treat this like business as usual, we'll fall short. The plan is designed to ignite something bigger—something transformative."

Jessica's eyebrow lifted. "Transformative is a strong word."

Tom nodded. "It is. And we chose it carefully. This BHAG isn't about incremental progress. It's about market leadership. It requires a mindset shift—not just from us but the whole organization."

Lisa added, "It's also about talent. The people involved in this sprint won't just help us hit the goal—they'll grow through it. Cross-functional collaboration like this builds capability *and* loyalty."

Mia spoke up, calm but firm: "This isn't just a business strategy. It's a cultural shift. A signal that we're not afraid to bet on bold thinking and back it up with bold action."

Jessica leaned back in her chair, folding her arms. "You've clearly put thought into this. But it's a big swing. Sprint weeks? Prioritization over other KPIs? Rethinking core workflows? Those aren't small asks. How do I know other departments will buy in?"

Karen didn't miss a beat. "Because we're going first. We've already begun dismantling what's not working and replacing it with what this goal demands. We're not asking for anything we haven't already committed to."

Jessica looked at her sharply. "And you think modeling that is enough?"

Sarah stepped forward, voice calm and clear. "It's a start. But we know this requires more. That's why we're not just presenting a plan but asking for your sponsorship. With your visible backing, we believe others will follow."

Jessica tapped her pen on the desk, thinking. "Okay. Let's say I back it. What's the first move?"

Lisa leaned in. "Sprint week. It creates momentum, alignment, and visibility across teams."

Tom added, "And we need conflicting KPIs paused for six months. This only works if the focus isn't fractured."

Karen nodded. "And decision-making autonomy at the team level. Speed only happens when trust flows top-down."

Jessica narrowed her eyes slightly. "You're asking me to take a risk."

WIN WITH GROWTH

Mia met her gaze. "And we're asking you to let us prove we've built a structure strong enough to carry it."

Jessica was quiet for a beat. "Bold ideas often fail in execution. What's your plan to stay on course?"

Karen answered first. "Accountability. We've set bi-weekly reviews with cross-functional updates. We've paired up as accountability partners. We've built in radical transparency. If something slips—you'll hear it from us first."

Jessica studied her. "You've come a long way, Karen. Have you considered leading this initiative?"

Karen didn't flinch. "Yes. I'm ready. But I'll need my team behind me—and your trust."

Sarah stepped beside her. "Karen's already leading. She's earned the team's confidence—and mine."

Karen looked at Sarah, emotion flickering behind her steady gaze. "Thank you. I won't waste this opportunity."

Jessica looked around the table, eyes lingering on each face. Then she set the document down and nodded slowly.

"All right. You have my support—but with one condition."

Everyone leaned in.

"I want tangible progress in 30 days. No theatrics. Just outcomes."

Tom nodded. "You'll have them."

Lisa smiled. "We've already started."

Jessica stood, signaling the meeting's close. "Good. You've got a window. Use it. Surprise me."

As the team exited the office, a restrained but unmistakable current of excitement passed between them.

"She said yes," Mia whispered.

Tom grinned. "Provisional, yes, sure. But still—momentum."

Lisa nodded, flipping her notebook shut. "Now we turn the pitch into proof."

Karen lingered behind. Sarah fell in step beside her.

"You were outstanding in there," Sarah said quietly.

Karen exhaled. "I was nervous. But I believed in what we were asking for. That made the difference."

Sarah smiled. "You're not just believing in the plan anymore. You're believing in *you*."

Karen's voice was quiet but confident. "Yeah. I think I finally am."

WIN WITH GROWTH

BEHAVIORS	ACCIDENTAL MANAGERS	LEVEL 10 LEADERS
What am I GETTING?	• Plateaued performance • Fear of failure or trying new things • A team stuck in their comfort zone	• A culture of curiosity, experimentation, and resilience • Team members who stretch beyond what they thought possible • Continuous improvement and shared learning
What am I DOING?	• Offering training but not opportunities • Focusing only on results, not progress • Avoiding failure instead of learning from it	• Applying the 10-20-70 rule: Learn – Observe – Do • Creating safe spaces to try, fail, and grow • Using See–Do–Get to reframe limiting beliefs
HOW am I SEEING?	• "Growth happens through promotions." • "Learning takes too much time right now." • "Some people just aren't growth-minded."	• "Growth is daily, not just annual." • "Stretch builds confidence and capability." • "Mindset shifts fuel behavior shifts."

LEVEL 10 LEADER

The One Thing Challenge – Win with GROWTH

Choose one team member—and turn a real business challenge into a growth opportunity.

Here's how:

1. **Start with a mindset shift (SEE):**

   Ask:

   "What limiting belief must we reframe to grow through this?"

2. **Create a development experience (DO):**

   Give them a real project or stretch assignment—not training.

   Use the **10-20-70 rule** to shape it:

   - 10% Learn (resource or insight)
   - 20% Coach (support through reflection)
   - 70% Do (on-the-job application)

3. **Reflect together (GET):**

   At the end of the week, ask:

   "What did you learn that you didn't know you could do?"

   Growth doesn't happen in theory.

   It happens in motion—and in mindset.

Your Next Move

Was this chapter helpful?

If it sparked a new insight or gave you a practical tool, take 30 seconds to leave a quick review.

Your words might be the reason another leader takes the first step.

☞ Leave a review on Amazon

Ready to grow from a reader to a Level-10 Leader?

Unlock Level 10 Leadership Assessment, Workbook and more at resources.level10leader.com

References

1. **Dweck, Carol S.** *Mindset: The New Psychology of Success.* Ballantine Books, 2007.

2. **Collins, Jim.** *Good to Great: Why Some Companies Make the Leap... and Others Don't.* Harper Business, 2001.

3. **Kirkpatrick, Donald L., and James D. Kirkpatrick.** *Evaluating Training Programs: The Four Levels.* Berrett-Koehler Publishers, 2006.

4. **Gallup Research.** "Why Accountability Improves Team Performance." Gallup, 2020.

5. **Lombardo, Michael M., and Robert W. Eichinger.** *The Career Architect Development Planner.* Lominger International (2009), the source of the 10-20-70 learning model.

6. **Edmondson, Amy C.** *The Fearless Organization: Creating Psychological Safety in the Workplace for Learning, Innovation, and Growth.* Wiley, 2018.

CHAPTER 7
Win With Delegation

"The greatest leader is not necessarily the one who does the greatest things. He is the one that gets the people to do the greatest things."

— Ronald Reagan.

"Before you are a leader, success is all about growing yourself. When you become a leader, success is about growing others."

— Jack Welch.

"The function of leadership is to produce more leaders, not more followers."

— Ralph Nader.

WIN WITH DELEGATION

Monday, June 2, 10:30 AM – Observation Deck, Riverside General Hospital

"Precision, Trust, and Letting Go"

Sarah stood just outside the observation deck of the hospital's surgical wing, furrowed with confusion as she looked through the large glass window into the bustling operating room below. Inside, a team of surgeons and nurses moved with precise coordination, the lead surgeon issuing quiet instructions.

She turned to Michael, who stood beside her with his hands in his pockets, a faint smile playing on his lips. "So, what's this about?" she asked, tilting her head toward the scene below. "Are you planning to teach me surgery now?"

Michael chuckled. "Not quite. But trust me—what you're about to see has everything to do with leadership."

Sarah raised an eyebrow but stayed silent, watching the lead surgeon, Dr. Harper, gestured to the younger surgeon beside her.

Dr. Harper's voice came through the intercom in the observation deck. "Patel, it's your turn. Take over for this next part."

Dr. Patel hesitated, her gloved hands hovering above the instruments. "This is delicate," she said, her voice carrying a hint of doubt.

Harper nodded. "That's why you're doing it. You've seen this procedure enough times to know what to do. I'll be here if you need me, but I trust you."

Sarah's eyes narrowed as she leaned closer to the glass. "Wait—she's handing over a critical part of the surgery? What if Patel messes up?"

Michael didn't answer immediately, letting her question hang in the air as Patel took a deep breath and began to work. Harper stayed close, her hands ready but relaxed, her voice calm as she occasionally offered subtle corrections.

"Good," Harper said. "Keep steady. You've got this."

As Patel moved through the procedure, Sarah noticed her hands becoming steadier, her confidence growing with each step. Harper's presence was reassuring but unobtrusive—a quiet safety net that let Patel lead without feeling micromanaged.

"That," Michael finally said, "is leadership."

Sarah glanced at him. "Letting someone take over something so critical? Isn't that risky?"

"Delegation always involves some risk," Michael replied. "But Harper isn't just offloading a task. She's practicing what Stephen Covey calls a win-win delegation."

Sarah tilted her head. "Win-win delegation?"

Michael nodded. "It's about creating outcomes where both the leader and the delegate benefit. Harper gains capacity by trusting Patel with this part of the surgery, freeing her to focus on the bigger picture. Patel gains experience and confidence, growing into a more capable surgeon. They both win and ultimately, so does the hospital."

WIN WITH DELEGATION

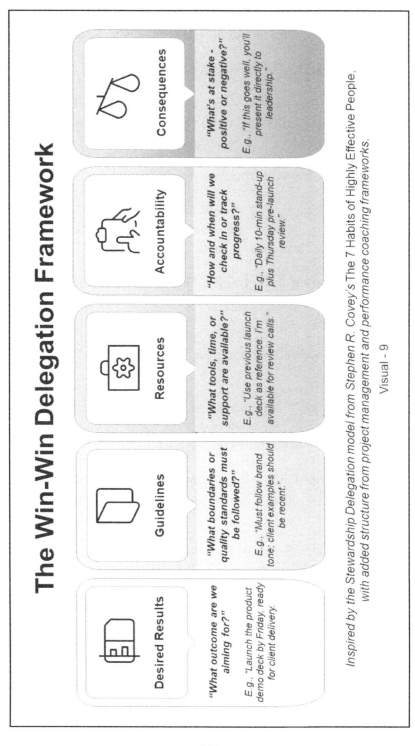

As they walked away from the observation deck, Michael turned to Sarah. "You've already done this, you know."

Sarah blinked. "Done what?"

"Win-win delegation. When you asked Karen to lead the project, you applied many of the principles we just saw."

Sarah hesitated, thinking back. "I did ask her to lead... but I'm unsure I followed through on everything."

Michael smiled. "Let's break it down. Covey's model has four elements: desired results, guidelines, resources, and accountability. How do you think you did on each?"

Sarah frowned thoughtfully. "For desired results, I think I was clear. I told Karen what needed to be achieved and why it was important."

Michael nodded. "That's a strong start. What about guidelines?"

"I'm not sure," Sarah admitted. "I wanted her freedom, so I didn't set too many parameters. Maybe I should've been clearer about where the boundaries were."

Michael tilted his head. "Sometimes less is more, but it depends on the person. Did Karen feel like she had enough direction?"

"I think so," Sarah said slowly. "She came to me with questions, and we worked through them together."

Michael smiled. "That sounds like you were a resource too. Did you make that explicit?"

"No," Sarah said, shaking her head. "I just assumed she'd come to me if she needed help."

"Good instinct," Michael said. "Finally, how did you handle accountability?"

Sarah hesitated. "I checked in with her regularly but didn't review the outcome with her in detail. I was just... relieved it was done."

Michael chuckled. "That's honest. So, what's your takeaway?"

Sarah exhaled slowly. "I think I did okay, but I could've been more deliberate. Clearer guidelines, more explicit support, and maybe a better feedback loop at the end."

Michael nodded. "And yet, it still worked. Karen grew, and you created capacity. Imagine how much more effective it could be with small tweaks. Win-win delegation is a skill like any other—it improves with practice."

Sarah smiled faintly. "It's reassuring to know I'm on the right track."

"You are," Michael said. "And your next opportunity to delegate is waiting. Just remember what you learned here—and what you've already done."

> *"Trust grows when expectations are clear. Delegation is not giving up control - it's giving others a chance to rise."*

LEVEL 10 LEADER

Friday, June 6, 3:00 PM – Sarah's Office, TechInnovate Headquarters

"The Conversation That Defines Ownership"

Sarah sat at her desk, flipping through her notebook. This wasn't about managing Karen—it was about empowering her. The six-month BHAG was ambitious, and Karen's leadership would be the linchpin. A knock at the door pulled her from her thoughts.

"Come in," Sarah called, standing as Karen entered.

"Hey, Sarah," Karen said, her tone neutral but with a hint of curiosity.

"Hi, Karen," Sarah said warmly, gesturing to the chair opposite her desk. "Thanks for making time. I wanted to sync up with you on the BHAG. We could use this time to determine how you see the path forward."

Karen took a seat, crossing her legs. "Sounds good. Where do we start?"

Sarah smiled and leaned forward. "You've already done the hard part—getting Jessica on board. Now that we have her support, I'd love to hear your thoughts on where we should focus first."

Karen paused, her expression thoughtful. "I think the cross-departmental alignment is the biggest hurdle. Without that, nothing else moves forward."

"Agreed," Sarah said, nodding. "Who do you think are the key players we need to engage?"

"Ravi, definitely," Karen said. "But also Priya in operations. She hesitates about automating workflows, which could slow us down."

"What approach do you think would work best with them?" Sarah asked.

Karen frowned slightly. "For Ravi, I think a one-on-one conversation might help. For Priya, we might need to show her data—proof that automation won't replace people but make their jobs easier."

"I like that," Sarah said, jotting down notes. "What resources or support do you need to make those conversations successful?"

Karen leaned back, her expression serious. "Time, for one. If we're going to automate workflows, we need to evaluate tools quickly but thoroughly. That's going to take focus."

Sarah nodded. "What do you think about involving the team in that process?"

Karen tilted her head. "It could work. They're more likely to buy in if they have a say."

"Exactly," Sarah said. "How do you want to structure that?"

Karen suggested, "Maybe we start with a demo from vendors. Then, the team can test the tools and give feedback before we commit."

"Great idea," Sarah said, writing it down. "Anything else you'd need from me or Jessica?"

Karen hesitated, then said, "Having Jessica back us up on prioritizing this across departments would help. If people know she's invested, they're more likely to get on board."

"I can coordinate with her on that," Sarah said. "What's the best way for you to keep me and Jessica in the loop?"

Karen shrugged. "Bi-weekly check-ins worked well during the planning phase. Maybe we stick with that for now?"

LEVEL 10 LEADER

"That works," Sarah said. "Do you think we need to adjust anything as the project progresses?"

"We might need more frequent updates for specific pieces, like the vendor demos," Karen said. "But we can decide that as we go."

"Perfect," Sarah said. "How do you feel about this plan so far?"

Karen smiled faintly. "I think it's coming together. Still a little daunting, but manageable."

Sarah leaned back and folded her hands. "Karen, this is your project. You've got the vision, the leadership, and the capability to make it happen. I'm here to support you however you need, but I trust you to drive this."

Karen's eyes softened, a flicker of pride breaking through her usual reserve. "Thanks, Sarah. That means a lot."

"And remember," Sarah added with a small smile, "I'll be the second happiest person in the room when we achieve this."

Karen chuckled. "I'll hold you to that."

As Karen left, Sarah exhaled deeply, feeling a quiet satisfaction. This wasn't about imposing ideas or control—it was about helping Karen realize her plan and giving her the space to lead. The delegation she was learning wasn't about handing off tasks. It was about handing over the trust.

WIN WITH DELEGATION

Wednesday, June 11, 11:00 AM – Small Conference Room, TechInnovate Headquarters:

"First Steps Towards Confidence"

Sarah sat at the small conference table, her notebook open to a fresh page. Across from her, Mia shifted nervously, a notepad clutched tightly in her hands. Mia, The youngest team member, had proven her technical skills in smaller tasks, but this would be her first chance to take on a project with broader responsibility.

"Thanks for meeting with me, Mia," Sarah began with a smile. "I've been thinking about the next steps for the BHAG, and I believe this is a great opportunity for you to lead part of the process."

Mia's eyes widened. "Me? Lead it? What kind of process?"

Step 1: *Define the Task Clearly*

Sarah flipped her notebook around to show a diagram. "We need to coordinate a feedback loop between our team and the pilot users testing the new workflow tool. You will design how we collect, organize, and present their input."

Mia bit her lip. "That sounds... big. What if I miss something?"

Sarah leaned in, her voice steady. "That's why I'm here to support you. Let's break it down: The first step is creating a simple survey for the users to share their thoughts. From there, you'll categorize and summarize the feedback for the team."

Step 2: *Match the Task to the Person*

As Mia studied the diagram, Sarah reflected on her decision. *Karen would have been more experienced with this type of work. Still, with her leading another initiative, this was a perfect chance for Mia to grow.*

Sarah had approached Karen differently—focused more on collaboration and strategic alignment. With Mia, the goal was skill-building, requiring a hands-on approach and structured guidance.

"You're the right person for this, Mia," Sarah said warmly. "You've been detail-oriented in your previous tasks, and your fresh perspective is exactly what we need to engage our pilot users."

Mia hesitated. "But I've never done anything like this before."

"That's why this is the perfect opportunity," Sarah said. "You'll learn as you go, and I'll be here to guide you."

Step 3: *Provide Clear Expectations*

Sarah turned to the timeline sketched in her notebook. "Here's how I see it: Draft the survey by Friday. Next week, we'll send it to users and start collecting feedback. At the end of the month, you'll present your findings to the team."

Mia nodded slowly, her confidence growing. "Okay. And what if the users don't respond?"

"That's part of the process," Sarah said. "Think of ways to follow up—email reminders or a quick call. Your job is to make it easy for them to engage."

Step 4: *Provide Necessary Support*

"I'll join you for the first meeting with the pilot users," Sarah continued. "I'll handle introductions, and then you'll take the lead. Afterward, we'll have weekly check-ins to ensure everything's on track."

Mia's posture relaxed slightly. "That sounds manageable."

"And if you hit any roadblocks before our check-ins, just reach out," Sarah said. "I'm here to support you, but I want you to drive this."

Step 5: *Establish Accountability*

Sarah slid a checklist across the table. "This is a breakdown of your key milestones. Send me a quick update at the end of each week—what's done, what's next, and any challenges."

Mia studied the checklist and nodded. "That works. I'll keep you updated."

"Great," Sarah said, closing her notebook. "How are you feeling about this?"

Mia smiled faintly. "Excited. Nervous, but excited."

As Mia left, Sarah leaned back in her chair, her mind drifting to her recent meeting with Karen. With Karen, delegation had been about empowerment—stepping back to let her shape the BHAG's strategy while offering minimal oversight. Karen's experience and confidence meant Sarah could focus on being a sounding board and strategic ally.

The approach with Mia was different. This was about developing skills and building confidence, requiring Sarah to provide more structure and support. She needed to balance giving Mia autonomy with ensuring she felt guided every step of the way.

Sarah thought delegation wasn't a one-size-fits-all skill, jotting a quick note in her journal. *With Karen, I focused on empowerment. With Mia, it's about nurturing growth. Matching the approach to the person and the situation makes it work.*

Sarah closed her notebook and exhaled, a small smile tugging at her lips. Delegation wasn't just about handing over tasks—it was about seeing the potential in others and giving them what they needed to succeed. It felt like leadership in its truest form.

LEVEL 10 LEADER

Monday, June 23, 10:00 AM – Jessica's Office, TechInnovate Headquarters:

"Delegation Unlocks Elevation"

Sarah sat across from Jessica in her sleek, minimalist office. The large windows offered a stunning view of the city skyline, but Sarah's eyes were on Jessica, who was flipping through a small stack of notes. The last time they'd sat like this was during one of the lowest points in Sarah's career—the aftermath of the disastrous town hall.

Back then, Jessica's words had been firm but supportive: *"Leadership is about weathering storms. Take time, reflect, and rebuild."* Sarah had clung to that advice like a lifeline. Now, months later, this meeting felt different. She had come far, but the echoes of those struggles still lingered.

"Thanks for making time, Sarah," Jessica said, breaking the silence. She placed her notes down and looked up, her expression steady but kind. "It feels like just yesterday we were having a very different conversation in this office."

Sarah smiled faintly, the memory of that day washing over her. "It does. A lot has changed since then."

Jessica nodded. "It has. And I want to take a moment to acknowledge that. You've made incredible progress—not just with your team, but with yourself. I can see it in how you're delegating, how you're trusting others, and how you're starting to own your leadership style."

The words landed surprisingly, and Sarah felt a lump rise in her throat. "Thank you," she said softly. "There were times I didn't think I'd get here."

Jessica leaned forward, her tone gentler now. "I know. And I'm proud of you for pushing through. But I also know you're not done yet. Leadership is a constant journey where the lessons never stop coming."

Sarah nodded, absorbing the truth in Jessica's words. "I'm starting to understand that."

Jessica nodded. "I can see that. And now, I think you're ready for the next challenge."

Jessica gestured to the folder. "We've been wrestling with a persistent issue—operational inconsistencies across teams. Different departments have different processes, reporting structures, and tools. It's creating inefficiencies that ripple across the company."

Sarah opened the folder and scanned its contents: fragmented workflows, communication gaps, and repeated complaints about duplicated efforts. It was a classic operations challenge, and its scale quickened her pulse.

Jessica continued. "I'd like you to take the lead on addressing this. Start by focusing on workflow alignment—bringing together department heads to map out redundancies and agree on a unified process. Once we have that foundation, we can roll it out across the organization."

Sarah's gaze lingered on the folder. She could already see the complexity of the task—the negotiations it would require, the pushback it might provoke. Months ago, she would have balked at the idea, certain that it was too much. But now?

Her thoughts drifted to her team. Karen confidently ran the BHAG, and her cross-departmental work set a strong example. Mia managed the pilot feedback loop independently, showing remarkable growth for someone so new. The team was thriving, and it was because Sarah had learned to delegate effectively to trust them.

LEVEL 10 LEADER

Jessica's voice broke through her thoughts. "I know this is a significant undertaking, but I wouldn't ask if I didn't believe you could handle it. Take some time to think it over. If you're in, we can discuss next steps."

Sarah nodded slowly, her fingers brushing the edge of the folder. "Thank you for trusting me with this. I'll need a little time to consider it."

Jessica smiled, her eyes glinting with approval. "Of course. Let me know by the end of the week. And whatever you decide, I want you to know that you've already proven yourself."

As Sarah left the office, the folder was clutched tightly in her hand, and she walked past her team's workstations. Karen was deep in conversation with another manager, her posture confident and composed. Mia sketched diagrams on a whiteboard, explaining something animatedly to a group of peers.

Sarah paused for a moment, taking in the scene. The weight of Jessica's challenge still sat heavily on her shoulders, but now, it didn't feel overwhelming.

They're thriving because I trusted them, she thought. *Because I let go of control and gave them room to grow. That's why I can even think about taking this on.*

She returned to her desk and set the folder down, her mind spinning with possibilities. For now, she'd let the idea sit, let the details marinate. But deep down, a quiet confidence was building.

I can do this—because I don't have to do it all.

Thursday, June 26, 3:30 PM – Break Room, TechInnovate Headquarters

"The Ripple Effect of Trust"

The soft hum of the coffee machine filled the break room as Karen leaned against the counter, hands wrapped around a steaming mug. Across the room, Tom scrolled through his phone, glancing up occasionally. Mia walked in, balancing a plate of cookies from the snack station, and right behind her, Lisa carried a small stack of napkins and her ever-present notepad.

"Perfect timing," Karen said, eyeing the cookies. "We needed something sweet after the morning we've had."

Mia grinned, setting the plate down. "Pilot feedback's rolling in—and let's just say, some of it stings."

Tom looked up with a smirk. "If no one's getting scorched, you're not pushing boundaries."

Lisa chuckled as she passed out napkins. "True. But wow, some of those comments were... brutally accurate."

Mia took a seat. "Honestly, though, I'm learning a lot. A few months ago, I wouldn't have believed I could handle something this complex."

Karen nodded. "Sarah's been good about that. She pushes, but she doesn't leave you stranded. You had structure, space, and support."

Mia smiled. "Exactly. Weekly check-ins and clear goals—but she let me figure things out my way. That kind of trust makes a difference."

Tom leaned back, sipping his coffee. "It's been the same for me. When Sarah first took over as Ops Manager, she was... let's say, a little too hands-on."

LEVEL 10 LEADER

Karen smirked. "That's generous."

Lisa laughed. "She's evolved. The BHAG is proof of that. Karen's leading, and Sarah's letting it happen—without hovering."

Karen nodded, more reflective now. "She's still there when I need her. She connects dots I hadn't seen—but she's not micromanaging. She's letting me own it."

Lisa leaned forward. "Maybe that's why things feel different lately. There's still pressure, but the tension's eased. It feels... collaborative."

Mia added, "It's like we've stopped bracing for impact. There's more flow—more trust."

Karen said, "That's what trust *does*. It changes how you show up—not just to get things done, but to prove you can lead."

Tom chimed in, his tone thoughtful. "And it's not just us stepping up—Sarah is, too. She's delegating because she's building something beyond the immediate. That's how real teams grow."

Karen glanced at the clock and stood, finishing her coffee. "Whatever comes next, we're in a stronger place. Sarah's learning. So are we."

Mia grabbed a cookie. "We're not just completing tasks anymore. We're building something meaningful."

Lisa raised her cookie like a toast. "To trust and transformation."

Tom gave a mock salute. "And cookies. Never underestimate cookies."

WIN WITH DELEGATION

Laughter echoed as they walked out together, the easy camaraderie a quiet testament to the culture they were co-creating. Sarah's trust wasn't just felt—it was fueling something bigger: a team becoming more than the sum of its parts.

LEVEL 10 LEADER

WIN WITH DELEGATION

BEHAVIORS	ACCIDENTAL MANAGERS	LEVEL 10 LEADERS
What am I GETTING?	• Bottlenecks and burnout • Team dependence on you for every decision • Stalled growth for both leader and team	• Increased capacity and confidence • Team members who lead with initiative • More time for strategic, high-impact work
What am I DOING?	• Micromanaging or taking work back • Delegating only tasks, not outcomes • Avoiding delegation out of fear of mistakes	• Delegating using the Win-Win Framework (Covey model) • Matching delegation style to readiness (Situational Leadership) • Empowering ownership while staying available for support
HOW am I SEEING?	• "If I want it done right, I have to do it myself." • "Delegation means losing control." • "It's faster if I just handle it."	• "Delegation is how I grow others and myself." • "Trust multiplies when I give it." • "Letting go is the path to scaling up."

The One Thing Challenge – Win with DELEGATION

Choose one high-impact task—and delegate it intentionally using the Win-Win Framework.

Here's how:

1. Select the right opportunity:
2. Pick a meaningful, visible, and growth-oriented task—not just a leftover one.
3. Use the Win-Win Delegation prompts:
4. Clearly define:
   - Desired Results
   - Guidelines
   - Resources
   - Accountability
   - Consequences

Then say the 7 most powerful words in leadership:

"I trust you. You've got this. I'm here."

Your Next Move

Was this chapter helpful?

If it sparked a new insight or gave you a practical tool, take 30 seconds to leave a quick review.

Your words might be the reason another leader takes the first step.

☞ Leave a review on Amazon

Ready to grow from a reader to a Level-10 Leader?

Unlock Level 10 Leadership Assessment, Workbook and more at resources.level10leader.com

References

1. Covey, Stephen R. *The 7 Habits of Highly Effective People.* Simon & Schuster, 1989.

2. Gallup Research. "The Impact of Employee Autonomy on Engagement." Gallup, 2020.

3. Edmondson, Amy C. *The Fearless Organization: Creating Psychological Safety in the Workplace for Learning, Innovation, and Growth.* Wiley, 2018.

4. Lencioni, Patrick. *The Five Dysfunctions of a Team: A Leadership Fable.* Jossey-Bass, 2002.

CHAPTER 8
Win With Feedback

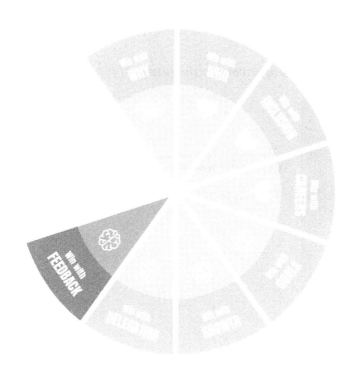

"Feedback is the breakfast of champions."
— Ken Blanchard

"Feedforward is the future of feedback."
— Marshall Goldsmith

"What gets measured gets managed."
— Peter Drucker

WIN WITH FEEDBACK

Monday, July 14, 3:30 PM – TechInnovate Headquarters, Parking Lot

"Signals, Speedometer, and a Shift"

The late afternoon sunlight bathed the office parking lot in a golden glow as Sarah climbed into Michael's car. He had stopped by for a visit and suggested a drive, offering no further explanation. Sarah, intrigued but wary, buckled her seatbelt and glanced at him.

"You're keeping me guessing," she said with a smirk. "What's the lesson this time?"

Michael laughed, starting the engine. "No lesson. It's just a drive. Let's see where it takes us."

They pulled out onto the main road, the quiet hum of the car filling the space. Michael gestured to the dashboard. "Let me ask you something: What do you look at the most when driving?"

Sarah raised an eyebrow, glancing at the speedometer. "The speedometer, I guess. And sometimes the fuel gauge."

"Why?" Michael asked, his tone casual.

"To make sure I'm not speeding—or about to run out of gas," Sarah replied with a shrug. "You don't want to ignore those things."

"Exactly," Michael said, nodding. "That's your internal feedback. It tells you if everything inside the car is running smoothly or if you need to adjust."

Sarah tilted her head, intrigued but unsure where he was going with this.

As they approached an intersection, Michael slowed for a red light. "Now look around. What else is giving you signals?"

"Traffic lights, stop signs, lane markers," Sarah said. "Other cars, I guess."

Michael smiled. "External feedback. Without it, we'd all be crashing into each other."

Sarah smirked. "Okay, I see where you're going. Driving is full of signals. But what's the point?"

Michael grinned. "Patience. We're getting there."

They turned onto a winding road lined with trees, the sunlight flickering through the branches. Michael tapped the GPS on the dashboard. "What about this? How often do you use a GPS when driving somewhere unfamiliar?"

"All the time," Sarah admitted. "It's easier than guessing. And if I take a wrong turn, it just reroutes me."

"Exactly," Michael said. "And does it ever get angry at you for missing a turn?"

Sarah laughed. "No, it just adjusts and tells me what to do next."

Michael nodded, his tone more reflective now. "Think about that for a second. The GPS doesn't blame you. It doesn't dwell on what you did wrong. It just helps you get back on track."

Sarah frowned slightly, a realization dawning. "You're talking about feedback, aren't you?"

Michael smiled his eyes on the road. "What do you think?"

As they continued driving, Michael glanced at Sarah. "Let me ask you this: Can you think of times in the past few months when you've acted on signals—feedback—without realizing it?"

Sarah thought for a moment. "Karen, for sure. She didn't say it outright, but her resistance early on was signaling that I was micromanaging. I adjusted, gave her more space, and now she's thriving."

Michael nodded. "Exactly. And Tom?"

Sarah smiled faintly. "His disengagement was feedback, too. Once I trusted him with more responsibility, he stepped up."

"And Mia?" Michael asked. "What did her hesitation tell you?"

"That she needed more structure and guidance," Sarah said, her tone more confident now. "Once I gave her that, she gained confidence."

Michael slowed as they approached a scenic overlook. "Do you see the pattern here? Feedback isn't always explicit. Sometimes, it's subtle, like a dashboard light or a GPS reroute. But it's always there if you're paying attention."

As they drove, Michael continued. "Let me explain why feedback has to come after trust. Think about this: If you had tried giving Karen or Tom constructive feedback back when they weren't fully on board with you, how do you think it would've gone?"

Sarah winced. "Not well. Karen would've pushed back harder, and Tom probably would've tuned me out completely."

"Exactly," Michael said. "Feedback without trust feels like criticism. But feedback in an environment of trust feels like guidance. It's a gift from a place of respect and shared goals."

Sarah nodded slowly. "So, feedback isn't just about what you say—it's about the relationship behind it."

Michael smiled. "Now you're getting it. You've already won their trust by empowering them. Now it's time to use feedback to deepen that trust and help them—and yourself—grow."

LEVEL 10 LEADER

A short drive later, they parked at a cozy café. Inside, the aroma of freshly brewed coffee filled the air as they settled into a quiet corner table. Sarah sipped her cappuccino, her curiosity piqued.

Michael leaned forward. "Let's get practical. Feedback can feel overwhelming, but there's a framework I like to use called CARS: *Context, Actions, Results, and Suggestions*. It gives feedback structure and makes it easier to give and receive."

WIN WITH FEEDBACK

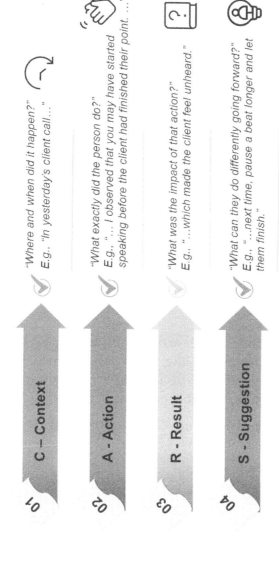

LEVEL 10 LEADER

1. **Context**

   "Start by setting the context," Michael said. "Describe the situation or project, like, 'In yesterday's team presentation...' This ensures the person understands the frame of reference."

   Sarah nodded. "So, no jumping straight to criticism. Start with where it happened."

   "Exactly," Michael said.

2. **Actions**

   "Then focus on actions," Michael continued. "Use 'I' statements to describe what you observed. For instance: 'I noticed how clearly you explained the technical details and answered the client's questions confidently.' This keeps the feedback specific and actionable without sounding accusatory."

   Sarah tilted her head. "It keeps things neutral and focused on behaviors."

   "Right," Michael said. "And it ensures the feedback feels constructive, not personal."

3. **Results**

   "Next, connect the actions to results," Michael said. "Explain the impact, like, 'Your clarity helped the client feel reassured, and they decided to move forward.' This ties their effort to a tangible outcome."

   Sarah tapped her mug. "That's motivating. It shows them their work matters."

   "Exactly," Michael said.

4. **Suggestions**

   "Finally, offer suggestions for improvement," Michael said. "For example: 'Next time, consider using visuals to simplify complex data.' This turns feedback into a growth opportunity."

Sarah leaned back, impressed. "CARS makes feedback practical and actionable."

Michael smiled. "The framework is great, but a few timeless principles make feedback even more effective."

1. **Feedback Should Be Timely**

"Address issues while they're fresh," Michael said. "If you wait too long, it loses relevance. Timely feedback helps people connect it to their actions."

Sarah nodded. "That makes sense. Waiting too long feels disconnected."

2. **Use 'I' Statements, Not 'You' Statements**

"Frame feedback constructively," Michael said. "'I noticed the presentation ran longer than expected,' which is better than 'You didn't manage your time well.' It makes the conversation less confrontational."

Sarah smiled. "So, it's about collaboration, not blame."

3. **Be Open to Dialogue**

"Feedback should be a conversation," Michael added. "Ask questions like, 'What do you think went well?' or, 'How do you see this improving?' Dialogue builds trust."

"That's a good reminder," Sarah said. "It's not a lecture — it's a partnership."

4. **Focus on Growth, Not Blame**

"Shift the focus to improvement," Michael said. "Instead of pointing out flaws, say, 'Here's what went well, and here's how we can make it even better.' Growth builds confidence."

Michael leaned in, his tone more reflective. "There's one more principle I want to share. It's called *Feedforward*. Marshall Goldsmith introduced it as an alternative to traditional feedback."

LEVEL 10 LEADER

Feedback vs. Feedforward: What's the Difference?

Feedback

- Focuses on the past
- Often tied to judgment or evaluation
- Can feel personal or threatening
- Sounds like: "Here's what went wrong"
- Triggers defensiveness

Feedforward

- Focuses on the future
- Anchored in growth and possibilities
- Feels collaborative and safe
- Sounds like: "Here's what could help next time"
- Invites reflection and creativity

Use feedback to learn from the past.
Use feedforward to shape the future.

Inspired by the Feedforward concept introduced by Marshall Goldsmith in What Got You Here Won't Get You There, as a future-focused alternative to traditional feedback.

Visual – 11

WIN WITH FEEDBACK

Sarah raised an eyebrow. "Feedforward?"

Michael nodded. "It's about focusing on the future, not the past. Instead of saying, 'You didn't delegate well on the last project,' you'd ask, 'What's one way you could empower your team more on the next project?' It shifts the conversation to possibilities rather than criticism."

Sarah sipped her coffee thoughtfully. "That feels... lighter. More optimistic."

"It is," Michael said. "Feedforward inspires action and builds momentum. It's particularly powerful when someone feels stuck or defensive about past mistakes."

Michael smiled. "You've already seen how feedback works, Sarah—Karen's resistance, Tom's disengagement, Mia's hesitation. Those were signals, and you acted on them intuitively. Now it's time to add intention with CARS and these principles."

Sarah hesitated. "But what if my team's hesitant to give feedback?"

Michael nodded. "That's where trust comes in. Start small. Ask for feedback on something low-stakes, like how you ran a meeting. Use CARS or Feedforward to model the process. Over time, your team will feel safe enough to share openly."

As they walked back to the car, Michael gestured toward the horizon. "Feedback is like the signals on the road. Pay attention, adjust, and you'll get where you're going. And with Feedforward, you're looking toward the road ahead, not the one behind."

Sarah smiled as they climbed into the car. "This all makes sense. CARS gives me structure, the principles make it actionable, and Feedforward shifts the focus to the future. Feedback isn't a threat—it's a guide."

Michael started the engine. "Exactly. Feedback is your next win, Sarah. Time to hit the road and make it part of your leadership."

Wednesday, July 16, 10:00 AM – Sarah's Office, TechInnovate Headquarter:

"Feedback in Action"

Sarah sat at her desk, a faint smile on her lips as she reviewed her notes. *"Feedback should be a conversation, not a lecture,"* Michael had said. She wanted her team to feel heard and to see feedback as an opportunity for growth, not criticism. Preparing for her 1:1s, she made a mental note to lead with questions and listen before offering her perspective.

Conversation 1: Feedback for Mia (Course Correction)

Mia entered the office, her notepad in hand. "Hi, Sarah. You wanted to see me?"

Sarah gestured to the chair. "Yes, Mia. I wanted to talk about the pilot feedback loop and hear your thoughts on how it's going."

Mia sat, her expression thoughtful. "It's been good overall. The survey responses were helpful, but I feel like some of the answers were... surface-level. I think we might need to dig deeper."

Sarah nodded. "That's a good observation. What ideas do you have for getting more detailed feedback?"

Mia hesitated, then said, "Maybe we could include more open-ended questions or even set up short interviews with some users."

"I love those ideas," Sarah said. "Adding interviews could give us richer insights. And I thought the same about open-ended questions—they could help us capture more nuance."

Mia smiled. "It would make the results more meaningful."

"Exactly," Sarah said. "You're doing a great job, Mia. These adjustments will make your work even stronger. Let's collaborate on the next round."

Conversation 2: Feedback for Tom (Reinforcing What's Working)

Tom leaned casually against the doorframe. "Hey, Sarah. What's up?"

Sarah smiled. "I wanted to check in on the operations workflow project. How do you think it's going so far?"

Tom sat down, his brow furrowing slightly. "It's going well overall. I think the team's starting to align, but it's been a lot of follow-up work on my end to keep everyone on track."

"That's a fair point," Sarah said. "How do you think we could make that easier?"

Tom thought for a moment. "Maybe we could use a shared tracker or tool so everyone knows what's going on without me chasing them."

Sarah nodded. "I think that's a great idea. A shared tracker could save you a lot of time. I was going to suggest something similar."

Tom leaned back, a small smile forming. "Alright, I'll check out some tools."

"Great," Sarah said. "You're leading this project so well, Tom. The way you've managed those tough conversations has made all the difference. Keep it up."

Conversation 3: Feedback for Karen (Course Correction)

Karen entered the office with her usual confidence. "What's on your mind, Sarah?"

Sarah leaned forward slightly. "I wanted to get in touch on the BHAG alignment work. How do you feel the meetings have been going?"

Karen tilted her head thoughtfully. "I think they're going well. We've gotten buy-in from most stakeholders, but I did notice some hesitation in the last meeting."

"What do you think might be causing that?" Sarah asked.

Karen shrugged. "Maybe some people aren't comfortable speaking up in the larger group."

"That's a possibility," Sarah said. "What do you think we could do to encourage more input?"

Karen's eyes lit up. "We could add a quick roundtable at the end, where everyone can share concerns or ideas."

"I love that," Sarah said. "It's exactly what I was thinking. Adding that structure could make a big difference."

Karen nodded. "I'll implement that for the next meeting."

"Great," Sarah said. "You've done incredible work so far, Karen. This adjustment will only make it better."

As Sarah finished her 1:1s, she felt a sense of accomplishment. She created collaborative and empowering conversations by inviting her team to share their ideas first. Feedback wasn't something she gave—it was something they built together.

Wednesday, July 23, 11:00 AM – Local Café, Downtown:

"Trust, Tea, and Truths"

The team sat around a sunlit patio table at a local café, their plates filled with sandwiches and salads. Karen had planned the outing as an informal break to recharge during a busy week. The buzz of conversation from nearby tables created a relaxed backdrop as the team settled in.

Karen sipped her iced tea and leaned back in her chair. "I needed this. The BHAG alignment is moving, but it's been... intense."

Tom nodded, spearing a piece of his salad. "Operations is no cakewalk either. But at least Sarah's helping keep things on track."

Mia glanced up from her sandwich. "You mean with feedback?"

Tom shrugged. "Yeah. It's different now. She's not just pointing things out—she's asking questions and listening. It feels... collaborative."

Lisa wiped her hands with a napkin. "Totally. During the sprint planning, she didn't critique my proposed timeline—she asked how confident I felt about it. That one question made me rethink everything."

Karen smiled. "I noticed that too. In our last alignment meeting, she suggested the roundtable idea after asking me how I thought things were going. It wasn't just her telling me what to do—it was a conversation."

Tom gestured with his fork. "Same here. When I mentioned how much follow-up I was doing, she didn't just suggest a tracker—she asked if I thought it would help. That made it easier to buy into."

Mia nodded. "She's doing the same with the pilot feedback loop. She didn't say, 'Change the survey.' She asked what I thought about the responses and where we could dig deeper."

Lisa added, "And when I missed a small detail in last week's report, she didn't make it a big deal. She just flagged it gently and asked if I needed help streamlining the process. That kind of support builds trust."

Karen chuckled. "It's funny—she's giving more feedback than ever, but it feels less like micromanaging and more like she's... invested."

Tom leaned back in his chair. "It's a big shift from when she first became Ops Manager. Back then, it felt like she was in every detail."

Karen nodded. "She's grown. Now, she's helping us find our way instead of steering everything herself."

Mia tilted her head. "You think that's why she asks us for feedback, too? Like, she's trying to lead by example?"

Lisa smiled. "Exactly. I think she's showing us how feedback should feel—honest, clear, and human. That's a game changer."

Karen leaned in. "It's not just about what she says—it's how she creates space for us to share, improve, and grow."

The waiter stopped by with refills, and the group paused to thank him. As the conversation picked up again, Mia spoke thoughtfully.

"I like most that Sarah's feedback doesn't feel like criticism. It's more like... guidance. Like she's showing us how to get better, not just pointing out flaws."

Lisa nodded. "Because of that, I've started giving better feedback, too. It feels less scary when it's modeled well."

Karen raised her glass. "Here's to feedback without micromanagement."

Tom laughed, clinking his glass against hers. "I'll drink to that."

The team laughed, and their camaraderie was easy and real. As they finished their lunch and gathered their things, the sense of trust and collaboration Sarah had nurtured lingered—a quiet but powerful reflection of leadership done right.

WIN WITH FEEDBACK

BEHAVIORS	ACCIDENTAL MANAGERS	LEVEL 10 LEADERS
What am I GETTING?	• Avoided conversations and unresolved tension • Frustration around repeated mistakes • A culture of guessing, not growing	• A team that values feedback as fuel for growth • Faster improvement and fewer surprises • Stronger trust, transparency, and resilience
What am I DOING?	• Holding back feedback to avoid conflict • Delivering feedback too late or too vaguely • Using feedback only as correction	• Giving timely, specific, behavior-based feedback (C.A.R.S.) • Asking for feedback and modeling openness • Using feedforward to focus on the future, not just the past
HOW am I SEEING?	• "Feedback makes people defensive." • "If it's not broken, don't bring it up." • "People should just figure it out."	• "Feedback is a gift—it helps us get better." • "Done well, feedback deepens trust." • "Leaders grow when they invite and give feedback well."

The One Thing Challenge – Win with FEEDBACK

Give one piece of meaningful feedback this week—using the C.A.R.S. model.

Here's how:

1. **Choose someone who stretched, struggled, or showed growth.**
2. **Deliver your feedback using C.A.R.S.:**
   - Context: "In yesterday's client meeting…"
   - Action: "…you asked a powerful question that shifted the conversation."
   - Result: "…it built trust and got the client to open up."
   - Suggestion: "Keep using that instinct—your listening is a strength."
3. **Add a feedforward question:**

"What's one thing you'd like to try differently next time?"

Feedback isn't just correction—it's connection.

One thoughtful comment can unlock someone's next level.

Your Next Move

Was this chapter helpful?

If it sparked a new insight or gave you a practical tool, take 30 seconds to leave a quick review.

Your words might be the reason another leader takes the first step.

☞ Leave a review on Amazon

Ready to grow from a reader to a Level-10 Leader?

Unlock Level 10 Leadership Assessment, Workbook and more at resources.level10leader.com

References

1. Goldsmith, Marshall. *What Got You Here Won't Get You There*. Hyperion, 2007.

2. Buckingham, Marcus, and Ashley Goodall. *Nine Lies About Work: A Freethinking Leader's Guide to the Real World*. Harvard Business Review Press, 2019.

3. Covey, Stephen R. *The 7 Habits of Highly Effective People*. Simon & Schuster, 1989.

4. Dweck, Carol. *Mindset: The New Psychology of Success*. Ballantine Books, 2006.

CHAPTER 9
Win With Coaching

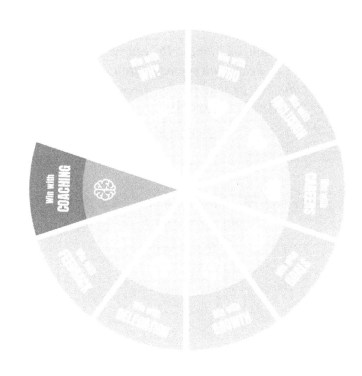

"There is no one best way to lead. The best way to lead is to adapt your style to the needs of the people you're leading."

— Ken Blanchard

"A coach is someone who tells you what you don't want to hear, helps you see what you don't want to see, so you can be who you've always known you could be."

— Tom Landry

"A good coach can change a game, but a great coach can change a life."

— John Wooden

Monday, August 11, 10:00 AM – Michael's Office, Downtown Palo Alto

"The Puzzle of Coaching"

Sarah entered the conference room to find a jigsaw puzzle across the table. Michael sat nearby, sipping his coffee and sorting pieces by color.

"A puzzle?" Sarah asked, raising an eyebrow. "Are we doing arts and crafts today?"

Michael grinned. "Not quite. This puzzle is going to teach us about coaching."

Sarah chuckled. "All right, let's see where this goes." She took a seat and picked up a handful of pieces.

As they began sorting the pieces, Michael asked, "How do you decide where a piece fits?"

"You look for the edges, the colors, the patterns," Sarah replied. "You try things until they click."

Michael nodded. "Exactly. Coaching works the same way. You observe, experiment, and adapt until you find the right fit. But what happens if you force a piece into the wrong spot?"

Sarah frowned, attempting to fit a piece that didn't belong. "You ruin the picture—or you waste time trying to make something work that never will."

"Exactly," Michael said. "That's what happens when we use the wrong coaching style for a team member's needs."

LEVEL 10 LEADER

Match Your Coaching Style to Their Growth Stage

LOW COMPETENCE → **HIGH COMPETENCE**

HIGH COMMITMENT / **LOW COMMITMENT**

DIRECTING STYLE
"I offer structure, timelines, and next steps."
"I need clear steps and direction."

COACHING STYLE
"I offer support, dialogue, and confidence-building."
"I need clarity and belief in myself."

DELEGATING STYLE
"I offer autonomy, availability, and trust."
"I need space to own this and stay trusted."

SUPPORTING STYLE
"I offer listening, trust, and shared decisions."
"I need encouragement and partnership."

Inspired by the Situational Leadership® Model by Ken Blanchard and Paul Hersey, adapted to coaching styles based on competence and commitment.

Visual - 12

Michael picked up a random puzzle piece and tried forcing it into an incorrect spot. "Let's say this piece is Mia. She's new and eager but unsure of the next steps. What do you think happens if you use a delegating style—'Figure it out yourself?"

"She'd probably feel overwhelmed and freeze," Sarah said, watching him struggle with the piece.

"Exactly," Michael replied. "She might lose confidence, disengage, or make costly mistakes because she didn't have the guidance she needed."

He picked another piece and tried fitting it into the wrong spot. "Now, let's take Karen. She's skilled, confident, and already leading the BHAG. What happens if you use a directive style with her?"

Sarah smirked. "She'd get frustrated—or feel micromanaged."

Michael nodded. "Right. Instead of helping, mismatched coaching creates friction, wastes energy, and can erode trust."

Michael picked up a puzzle piece, studied it carefully, and easily placed it into its correct spot. "Now, what happens when you match your coaching style to what a person needs? Let's go back to Mia. What happens if you use a directive style that gives her clear guidance and structure?"

Sarah picked up a similar piece and placed it. "She feels supported. She gains confidence."

"Exactly," Michael said. "And Karen? With a delegating style, you give her the space to own her work. She thrives."

Sarah leaned forward, adding a few more pieces to the growing puzzle. "So, it's all about observation—figuring out what they need and adjusting my approach."

Michael smiled. "That's the heart of *Situational Leadership*. Coaching is about helping people progress based on readiness, not forcing them to fit your style."

As they completed the puzzle, Michael gestured toward the final image. "Coaching, like this puzzle, is about alignment. The better you map where your team members are and match your approach to their needs, the faster and stronger everything comes together."

Sarah studied the finished picture, a sense of clarity settling over her. "It's not just about giving feedback or delegating. It's about meeting people where they are—and helping them move forward."

Michael handed her the box lid with the completed picture. "Exactly. And when you match well, you build trust, confidence, and results."

Sarah smiled. "Thanks, Michael. I think I've got my next challenge—and the tools to tackle it."

Tuesday, August 12, 9:00 AM – Conference Room, TechInnovate Headquarters:

"BHAG Reality Check"

The team gathered in the conference room, Karen standing at the head of the table. Sarah sat to the side, her notebook open to capture observations. Jessica had called this meeting to review progress on the BHAG and provide feedback on the team's direction.

Karen began with her usual confidence. "Thanks for making time, everyone. I'll start with an update on where we stand. We've secured buy-in from all stakeholders and outlined priorities for the next phase. The key focus areas are cross-departmental workflows, automation pilots, and capacity building."

She gestured to a slide on the screen. "Each area has a lead, and we've set preliminary milestones for each."

Tom leaned forward. "The automation pilot is underway. We've started getting feedback from operations, and while it's early, they seem cautiously optimistic."

Mia added, "On the capacity-building side, I'm finalizing changes to the feedback loop. The next round of user data should give us actionable insights."

Karen nodded. "And for workflows, we've begun drafting a detailed process map to align departments. We're planning to finalize it next week."

Jessica listened attentively, nodding at key points before leaning back in her chair. "First, let me commend all of you. You've made significant progress. The energy and collaboration I'm seeing are a big improvement from where we started. That's a testament to the trust you've built and the work you've done."

Karen smiled, and the team exchanged small nods. But Jessica's tone shifted slightly as she continued. "That said, I need to be candid. While the foundation is strong, we're not moving fast enough. Based on the timeline, we're off track to deliver the BHAG."

Karen frowned slightly. "Can you help us understand where we're falling short?"

Jessica gestured to the screen. "The areas you've identified—automation, workflows, capacity building—are the right priorities. But what's missing is execution at pace. Discussions are productive, but they're not translating into actionable results quickly enough."

LEVEL 10 LEADER

She scanned the room, her tone firm but constructive. "For example, the workflow alignment—finalizing it next week is fine, but when does implementation begin? And what's the timeline for scaling the automation pilot once initial feedback is in?"

Karen glanced at her notes, nodding slowly. "You're right. We've focused on alignment and planning but need to accelerate execution."

Tom added, "I think part of it is hesitation—some of us are waiting for perfect information before making decisions."

Mia looked thoughtful. "And on my end, I've been refining the process so much that I haven't started implementing anything yet."

Jessica leaned forward, her tone encouraging. "Exactly. Alignment is critical, but it has to lead to action. Planning is important, but don't let it paralyze you. Done is better than perfect in many cases."

Jessica addressed Karen directly. "Karen, you're leading this project well, but I'd like you to work with the team to revisit the plan. Focus on prioritizing immediate actions and setting shorter-term milestones to create momentum."

Karen nodded. "Understood. We'll regroup and refine the plan."

Jessica glanced at the rest of the team. "I know you're capable of delivering this BHAG. You've laid the groundwork—now it's time to start building on it."

As the meeting wrapped up, Sarah stayed quiet, absorbing the feedback. Jessica's message was clear: the team had the talent and the foundation, but execution needed to accelerate. Reworking the plan was the next step, and Sarah could already see where her role would come into play in supporting Karen and the team.

Karen gathered her notes, her expression determined. "Alright, team. Let's regroup tomorrow morning and determine how to pick up the pace."

The team nodded in agreement, the tension giving way to a shared sense of purpose.

Wednesday, August 13, 10:00 AM – TechInnovate Headquarters

"Rebuilding Karen's Confidence"

The morning sunlight streamed through Sarah's office window as Karen stepped in, her notebook tucked under her arm. Her usual confidence seemed tempered by uncertainty—a reflection of Jessica's feedback during the BHAG review.

Sarah gestured toward the chair across from her desk. "Come in, Karen. Thanks for making time. I thought we could take a moment to talk about reworking the plan and how we can best move forward."

Karen sat down, setting her notebook on her lap. "Sure. I've been thinking about Jessica's feedback, and honestly... I feel like I've let the team down. I should have seen this coming."

Sarah leaned forward, her voice steady and calm. "Karen, let me stop you right there. You haven't let anyone down. You've been leading this project with focus and determination, and our progress is because of your hard work."

Karen frowned, her shoulders sagging slightly. "It doesn't feel that way. Jessica's right—we're not moving fast enough. Maybe I'm not pushing the team hard enough."

Sarah shook her head. "You've been balancing trust and collaboration beautifully. Speeding up the pace isn't about pushing harder—it's about making small adjustments to how we work."

Karen sighed, flipping open her notebook. "I just keep second-guessing myself. Am I making the right decisions? Am I setting the right priorities? Sometimes it feels like I'm juggling too many things and don't know what to focus on."

Sarah nodded, her tone empathetic. "That's completely normal, Karen. Leadership isn't about having all the answers—it's about navigating the uncertainties and finding the path forward. What do you think is holding us back the most right now?"

Karen thought for a moment. "I think the alignment meetings are taking too long. We spend so much time discussing things, but we're not leaving with clear action steps. It's like we're stuck in planning mode."

"That's a great insight," Sarah said, her voice energizing. "You've already nailed the hard part—getting people to the table and on the same page. Now, it's about translating that into action. What do you think could help streamline the meetings?"

Karen hesitated, then said, "Maybe we need stricter agendas and clear task deadlines."

"I think that's a fantastic idea," Sarah said, leaning forward slightly. "And Karen, the fact that you're identifying these solutions shows you have the skills to lead this. You don't have to doubt yourself—you're doing better than you realize."

Karen exhaled, a small smile breaking through. "Thanks, Sarah. That's good to hear. Sometimes, it feels like I'm just spinning my wheels."

"What if we take it a step further?" Sarah suggested. "Could a shared project tracker help? Something visible to everyone that lists tasks, deadlines, and owners. That way, you're not carrying the entire burden of follow-up."

Karen's eyes lit up. "That could work. If the team sees the big picture, it might keep us all aligned and reduce the need for many discussions."

"Exactly," Sarah said. "And it reinforces accountability while freeing you up to focus on the bigger picture."

Karen jotted down notes. "I'll start looking into options for that. It could make a big difference."

Sarah smiled. "Karen, you've got this. You've been leading with clarity and focus, and the team trusts you because you've earned it. These adjustments aren't about fixing anything but amplifying what's already working."

Karen's shoulders relaxed, and she sat up straighter. "Thanks, Sarah. I needed this—it helps to talk it through."

Sarah nodded. "Anytime. You're not alone in this. Let's regroup next week to check how things are going."

Karen stood, her confidence visibly restored. "Will do. And thanks again—I feel like I can do this."

As Karen left, Sarah leaned back in her chair, a sense of satisfaction settling over her. Coaching, she realized, wasn't about providing answers—it was about helping people rediscover their strength.

LEVEL 10 LEADER

Thursday, August 14, 9:00 AM– TechInnovate Headquarters

"Mia's Moment of Clarity"

The faint hum of activity in the office provided a backdrop as Mia stepped into Sarah's office. She clutched a tablet, her expression uncertain. Sarah gestured toward the chair across from her desk.

"Come on in, Mia. I wanted to discuss the pilot feedback loop and how we're moving forward."

Mia nodded, sitting down and setting the tablet on her lap. "Thanks. I've been working on it, but I'm unsure if I'm focusing on the right things."

Sarah leaned forward slightly, her tone calm but firm. "You've made great progress with the user surveys, Mia. Your presentation last week was clear and well-structured. But, I noticed that we're still waiting on a detailed plan for the next round of feedback. What's holding you back?"

Mia hesitated. "I think... I'm just not sure how to structure it. Should I focus more on the technical feedback or the user experience? And what format would be best?"

"That's fair," Sarah said, nodding. "Here's how I think we should approach it. For this round, let's focus on the user experience first—where we'll get the most actionable insights. Use the same survey format as last time, but add three open-ended questions about ease of use and functionality. Can you do that?"

Mia nodded quickly. "Yes, I can do that. That helps a lot."

"Great," Sarah continued. "Once the survey responses start, prioritize categorizing the feedback into themes like navigation, clarity, and workflow. We'll use those categories to guide the follow-up interviews. Does that make sense?"

Mia jotted notes on her tablet. "It does. Focus on user experience, add open-ended questions, and categorize the feedback."

Sarah leaned back slightly. "I'll need the updated survey draft by Friday so we can review it together before it goes out to the users next week. Do you think that timeline works for you?"

Mia nodded. "Yes, I can do that."

"Good," Sarah said. "And remember, you don't have to figure everything out alone. If you hit any roadblocks while drafting, send me a quick note, and we'll work through it."

As Mia finished writing, Sarah added, "Mia, you're doing a great job. You've shown you're thoughtful and detail-oriented, which is why I know you can handle this. The clearer the plan, the easier to get the insights we need."

Mia smiled faintly, her shoulders relaxing. "Thanks, Sarah. I feel a lot more confident now."

"Good," Sarah said. "Let's touch base Friday, and we'll go over the survey draft together."

As Mia left, Sarah leaned back in her chair, feeling accomplished. Directive coaching, she realized, wasn't about micromanaging—it was about providing clarity and structure when someone needed it most. With a clear path forward, Mia now had the confidence to execute.

LEVEL 10 LEADER

WIN WITH COACHING

BEHAVIORS	ACCIDENTAL MANAGERS	LEVEL 10 LEADERS
What am I GETTING?	• A team that waits for answers • Short-term compliance, but low ownership • Missed opportunities for growth	• Team members who think, act, and grow independently • Deeper engagement and stronger confidence • A culture of shared learning and self-leadership
What am I DOING?	• Giving advice or instructions for every problem • Jumping in to fix things too quickly • Using one-size-fits-all management	• Matching coaching style to readiness (Situational Leadership) • Asking more, telling less • Creating space for reflection, experimentation, and ownership
HOW am I SEEING?	• "My job is to solve problems." • "People should already know what to do." • "If they're not asking, they must not need help."	• "My job is to grow people who solve problems." • "Everyone develops at their own pace." • "Coaching is how I build capability, not dependency."

The One Thing Challenge – Win with COACHING

Pick one team member—and adjust your leadership style to match their development level.

Here's how:

1. **Ask yourself:**

   "Where is this person on this task—new and eager (D1), struggling (D2), capable but cautious (D3), or confident and consistent (D4)?"

2. **Match your coaching approach:**

   - **D1:** Give clear direction and structure.
   - **D2:** Add encouragement and clarify the path.
   - **D3:** Ask questions. Build confidence. Share ownership.
   - **D4:** Step back. Trust them. Stay available.

3. **End with a growth question:**

   "What support would help you feel even more confident here?"

Coaching isn't one style—it's choosing the *right support* at the *right time* for the *right person*.

Your Next Move

Was this chapter helpful?

If it sparked a new insight or gave you a practical tool, take 30 seconds to leave a quick review.

Your words might be the reason another leader takes the first step.

☞ Leave a review on Amazon

Ready to grow from a reader to a Level-10 Leader?

Unlock Level 10 Leadership Assessment, Workbook and more at resources.level10leader.com

References

1. Blanchard, Ken. *The One-Minute Manager.* Harper & Row, 1982.

2. Dweck, Carol. *Mindset: The New Psychology of Success.* Ballantine Books, 2006.

3. Goldsmith, Marshall. *What Got You Here Won't Get You There.* Hyperion, 2007.

CHAPTER 10
Win With Rewards

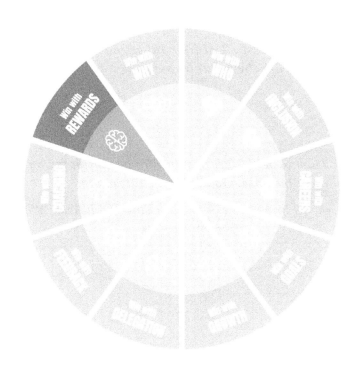

"People work for money but go the extra mile for recognition, praise, and rewards."
— Dale Carnegie, How to Win Friends and Influence People

"You get the best effort from others not by lighting a fire beneath them, but by building a fire within."
— Bob Nelson

"Human beings are designed to be motivated by purpose, mastery, and autonomy."
— Daniel Pink, Drive: The Surprising Truth About What Motivates Us

WIN WITH REWARDS

Saturday, September 20, 4:00 PM – Community Garden, Eastside Neighborhood

"The Garden Always Knows"

The late afternoon sun cast a golden glow over the community garden as Sarah stepped through the gate. Rows of vibrant plants stretched before her, their colors vivid and lush. Michael was crouched near a raised bed, carefully pruning a row of herbs.

Sarah approached with a smile. "I hope this isn't another metaphor about weeds."

Michael grinned, straightening. "Not weeds—growth. And, more importantly, how you recognize it. Grab a basket. We're harvesting today."

Michael gestured to the thriving garden around them as Sarah picked a ripe tomato and placed it in her basket. "Think of this garden as your team. Each plant represents someone's effort, skill, and potential. The work you've done—watering, weeding, nurturing—has brought it all to life."

Sarah tilted her head, intrigued. "And the harvest?"

Michael held up a squash. "That's the reward. It's how you show the plants—and in your case, your team—that their effort is noticed and valued. But here's the catch: just like plants need different care, people need different rewards."

Michael set the squash in his basket and turned to Sarah. "And you've already been doing this, whether you realize it or not."

Sarah blinked. "Really?"

"Absolutely," Michael said. "Take Karen, for example. You've given her autonomy—letting her lead the BHAG. That's recognition through trust, and she's thriving because of it."

Sarah smiled faintly. "I guess I never thought of it as a reward."

"It is," Michael said. "And Mia? You've challenged her to grow her skills while giving her clear guidance. That's feeding her need for mastery."

"And Tom?" Sarah asked, her curiosity growing.

Michael nodded. "With Tom, you've been showing him how his work connects to the bigger picture. That's the purpose. Every time you help him see the impact of his efforts, you're motivating him."

Michael moved to another row of plants, brushing his hand over the leaves. "Daniel Pink's AMP model—Autonomy, Mastery, and Purpose—explains why your approach has worked. People are motivated when their efforts are recognized in ways that align with what they value."

1. **Autonomy**

    "For someone like Karen, who thrives on ownership, the best reward is giving her space to lead without micromanaging."

2. **Mastery**

    "Mia lights up when she's learning and improving. The challenges you've given her and your guidance make her feel like she's growing."

3. **Purpose**

    "And Tom? He needs to feel like his work matters. You fuel his motivation whenever you connect his efforts to the BHAG's bigger goals."

WIN WITH REWARDS

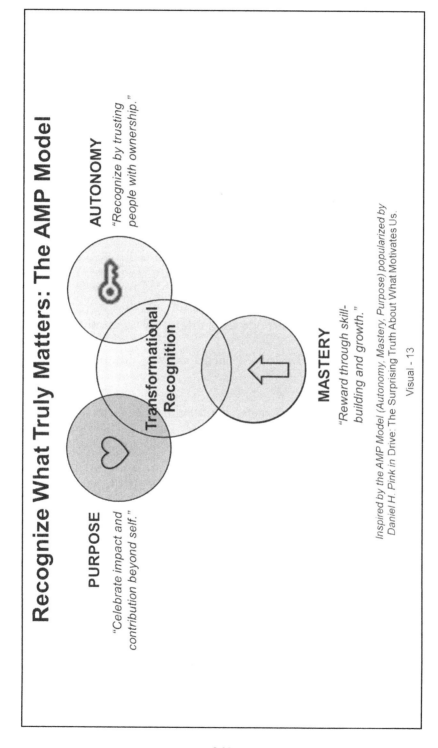

Michael gestured toward a few wilted plants in the corner of the garden. "But here's the thing: rewards aren't one-and-done. They'll struggle if you consistently forget to water or feed these plants."

Sarah frowned. "So, you're saying I need to keep recognizing them?"

"Exactly," Michael said. "Recognition isn't just about big milestones—it's about small, consistent rewards that keep the momentum going. A quick 'thank you,' a public shout-out, or even a conversation where you acknowledge their effort can go a long way."

Michael picked up a basket of fertilizer. "And one more thing—rewards have to match the person. If you give everyone the same generic reward, it loses meaning. It's like overwatering a cactus. What works for one might demotivate another."

Sarah chuckled. "So, I need to be intentional with rewarding them."

Michael nodded. "Exactly. Tailor the reward to the person and the effort. That's how you keep them engaged and growing."

As they finished harvesting, Sarah looked out over the garden. "You know, I've been so focused on pushing toward the BHAG that I haven't thought much about how I'm recognizing the team along the way."

Michael smiled. "You've been doing it instinctively. Now, you just need to make it intentional."

Sarah set her basket down, determination flickering in her eyes. "Autonomy, mastery, purpose. I've got it. Time to start harvesting—and rewarding."

Monday, September 29, 4:00 PM – TechInnovate Conference Room, Headquarters

"The Win That Matters Most"

The team gathered in the largest conference room, buzzing with excitement. The BHAG had been achieved, and Jessica had called this meeting to reflect on the journey and celebrate the milestone. The table was dotted with snacks and drinks, a rare treat that hinted at the occasion's significance.

Jessica stood at the head of the room, smiling as she surveyed the team. Sarah sat near Karen, Tom, Mia, and Lisa. Her pride was evident but tempered by curiosity about Jessica's message.

Jessica raised her glass of sparkling water. "First, let me say this: Congratulations. You did it. Not only did we hit the BHAG, but we exceeded expectations—and that's because of the incredible effort, collaboration, and commitment from everyone in this room."

The team broke into applause, exchanging smiles and nods. Jessica let the moment settle before continuing.

"This wasn't just a win for the project. This is a win for us as a team and as a company. And it's a win that will ripple through our culture and business."

Jessica gestured toward the screen, which displayed a timeline of the BHAG journey.

"This was no small feat. It started with alignment—Karen, you led those meetings with precision and focus. You created clarity where there was ambiguity, giving us a strong foundation."

Karen smiled, a hint of pride showing. "Thank you."

"Mia," Jessica continued, "your work on the user feedback loop didn't just refine the tool—it helped us create something already getting rave reviews from stakeholders. Your attention to detail and willingness to learn were pivotal."

Mia blushed, murmuring a soft "Thanks."

"And Tom," Jessica said, turning toward him, "you reminded us of why we're doing this. You brought purpose to every step of the process, keeping the team motivated when things got tough."

Tom smiled. "It was a team effort."

Jessica turned toward Lisa next. "Lisa—your ability to see across functions and anticipate what was needed before others saw it was critical. Your calm under pressure and how you lifted the energy in every room made a difference more than I can count."

Lisa beamed. "I'm just grateful to be part of something this meaningful."

Jessica nodded. "And Sarah—your leadership brought it all together. You trusted your team, gave them space to lead, and recognized their contributions at every turn. That's what empowered this group to deliver something extraordinary."

Jessica's tone grew more passionate.

"This BHAG proves what we can achieve when we come together with purpose and focus. It's not just a win—it's a *blueprint*. For how we take on challenges, build trust, and scale what works."

She looked around the room, her gaze steady. "Let's use this as a launchpad—not just for what we do, but for who we are. A culture of collaboration, recognition, and growth doesn't just happen—it's built. And you've already started laying the foundation."

Jessica raised her glass again, her smile warm.

"Here's to the BHAG—and to what comes next. Thank you for your hard work, dedication, and belief in what we can achieve together."

The team echoed the toast. Laughter and cheers filled the room. Sarah exchanged a glance with Karen and Lisa—each smiling, the weight of the journey replaced by a shared sense of pride and possibility.

As the celebration continued, Sarah stepped aside momentarily, watching the room come alive with stories, hugs, and well-earned joy. She took a deep breath, letting it all soak in.

This wasn't just a win, she thought. It was a **turning point**.

Jessica's right. The culture we've built here—it's real now. And it will shape everything we do from here on out.

Thursday, October 2, 7:00 PM – Cozy Local Restaurant, Downtown

"The Harvest"

The restaurant's private dining room glowed with soft ambient lighting, filled with the low hum of conversation and the occasional clink of silverware. A fire crackled gently in the corner, casting a golden warmth across the table. The long wooden table was set simply but elegantly—candles flickered between shared plates and glasses, and laughter bubbled up as the team eased into the evening.

Sarah had organized the dinner to celebrate the achievement of the BHAG and to honor the grit, heart, and growth each team member had shown. Karen, Tom, Mia, and Lisa sat around the table, already trading inside jokes and memories from the year.

LEVEL 10 LEADER

It had been a demanding ride, but tonight felt light.

Tom raised his glass, grinning. "So, team—we hit the BHAG. Does this make us legends now? Maybe we get a secret handshake? Or better yet, a trophy shaped like a Gantt chart?"

Karen smirked. "Forget the trophy. I want a statue—right in the lobby, with lighting and dramatic music when someone walks past."

Mia laughed, pushing her plate aside. "How about we start with dessert? Statues can wait until after the cake."

Lisa added, "I'd settle for a break from Monday morning metrics reviews. That's all the reward I need."

Sarah chuckled. "Alright, alright. I hear you. But since we're on the topic of recognition, I've got something for each of you. Just a small token of appreciation."

She reached down and brought up a tray of small gift boxes—elegant, simple, and meaningful.

She handed the first to **Karen**, who opened it to reveal a polished brass compass, engraved with the words: **"Guiding the Way."**

"Karen," Sarah said, "you were the compass for this project. You created clarity in moments of confusion. You helped this team stay aligned when the path was foggy. You led not just with direction—but with conviction."

Karen turned the compass over in her hand, her voice quiet. "Thank you. I'll carry this with me."

Next, Sarah handed a box to **Mia**. Inside was a delicate silver keychain shaped like a **ladder**.

"Mia, you grew with every challenge. You took on more, stretched yourself, and brought depth to everything you touched. This ladder symbolizes how far you've come—and how much further you're capable of going."

Mia's eyes lit up. "That's perfect. Thank you, Sarah."

Then Sarah turned to **Tom**, handing him a handcrafted lightbulb paperweight engraved with: **"Illuminating Purpose."**

"Tom, you brought heart and clarity to this entire journey. You helped all of us see why the work mattered—especially when things got tough. This lightbulb represents the insight and motivation you sparked across the team."

Tom grinned. "Finally—proof I'm full of bright ideas."

Sarah looked toward **Lisa**, and handed her a sleek wooden puzzle box, each side engraved with interlocking lines. On the base, it read: **"Connecting the Dots."**

"Lisa, you were the connector who saw how everything fit together before the rest of us could. You linked ideas, teams, and moments that might have been missed. This box is a reminder of your clarity, calm, and constant contribution."

Lisa smiled, tracing the lines. "This is beautiful. Thank you."

Karen set her compass down gently. "Sarah, you've spent all year reflecting on our growth. But you've grown too."

Mia nodded. "You believed in us from the beginning. But lately, we've seen you let go—trust us in new ways. And that trust made us rise."

Tom leaned forward. "You've gone from managing to leading. Not just by steering—but by creating space. This team? It's stronger because of you."

LEVEL 10 LEADER

Lisa added, "You didn't just guide the project. You transformed the way we work—and the way we see ourselves."

Sarah blinked, clearly moved. "Thank you. That means more than you know. This journey isn't just about what we achieved—it's about who we became."

Karen raised her glass again, grinning. "Alright. But if you ever leave us, just know—I'm using this compass to find you."

Mia laughed. "And I'm climbing the ladder right behind her."

Tom held up his lightbulb. "Someone's got to keep the lights on."

Lisa smiled, holding up the puzzle box. "And I'll be the one connecting the dots."

The table erupted in laughter. Sarah smiled, her eyes shining.

"You're not getting rid of me," she said. "We've built something here. Let's keep building."

WIN WITH REWARDS

WIN WITH REWARDS

BEHAVIORS	ACCIDENTAL MANAGERS	LEVEL 10 LEADERS
What am I GETTING?	• Recognition that feels generic or transactional • A team that feels overlooked or underappreciated • Low morale despite good performance	• Deepened motivation and connection • A culture of celebration and appreciation • Team members who feel truly seen and valued
What am I DOING?	• Rewarding only outcomes or top performers • Using the same incentives for everyone • Recognizing in ways that feel impersonal	• Celebrating growth, effort, and character—not just results • Using the AMP model (Autonomy, Mastery, Purpose) to personalize recognition • Making appreciation visible, timely, and symbolic
HOW am I SEEING?	• "Recognition is HR's job." • "If people want praise, they should work harder." • "Bonuses and promotions are enough."	• "Rewards are how I reinforce what matters most." • "People grow when they feel valued." • "A personalized thank you can change someone's belief in themselves."

LEVEL 10 LEADER

The One Thing Challenge – Win with REWARDS

Recognize one team member this week—not by telling them what you saw, but by trusting them with what comes next.

Here's how:

1. **Recognize with Autonomy**

   Don't just say thank you—*show* trust.

   Give them greater ownership, a visible role, or space to lead.

   "You've earned the freedom to shape how we move forward here."

2. **Reward through Mastery or Purpose**

   Choose a way to reinforce what matters most to them:

   - **Mastery:** Offer a learning opportunity, mentorship, or challenge stretch
   - **Purpose:** Acknowledge how their work connects to a larger mission or team impact

3. **Make it meaningful, not mechanical**

   Skip the generic praise. Say something like:

   "This isn't just about what you delivered—it's about who you're becoming."

   The best leaders don't just hand out rewards.

   They hand over belief, ownership, and opportunity.

Your Next Move

Was this chapter helpful?

If it sparked a new insight or gave you a practical tool, take 30 seconds to leave a quick review.

Your words might be the reason another leader takes the first step.

☞ Leave a review on Amazon

Ready to grow from a reader to a Level-10 Leader?

Unlock Level 10 Leadership Assessment, Workbook and more at resources.level10leader.com

References

1. Pink, Daniel. *Drive: The Surprising Truth About What Motivates Us*. Riverhead Books, 2009.

2. Dweck, Carol. *Mindset: The New Psychology of Success*. Ballantine Books, 2006.

3. Gallup, Inc. *StrengthsFinder 2.0*. Gallup Press, 2007.

PART-4

CLOSING

CHAPTER B
Another Townhall

"It's not how you start, it's how you finish that counts."
— Zig Ziglar

"The journey is the reward."
— Steve Jobs

"What lies behind us and what lies before us are tiny matters compared to what lies within us."
— Ralph Waldo Emerson

ANOTHER TOWNHALL

Wednesday, December 10, 10:00 AM – Thompson Residence

"A Sense of Deja-Vu"

The soft hum of conversation and the clinking of silverware filled Sarah's kitchen as she set plates on the table. The scent of roasted vegetables wafted through the air, mingling with the quiet chatter of her husband, Alex, and their daughter, Lucy, who was busy coloring at the dining table.

It was a calm scene, but inside Sarah, a storm brewed. Tomorrow loomed large in her mind—the annual day at TechInnovate, culminating a year's work and growth. And with it came the memories of the town hall that had shaken her to her core.

As they settled into dinner, Alex noticed her distant expression. "Penny, for your thoughts?" he asked, his tone light but probing.

Sarah managed a faint smile. "Just thinking about tomorrow," she said, twirling her fork in her salad. "And… the last time I stood in front of everyone."

Alex's face softened, and Lucy looked up curiously. "Mama, are you nervous?" Lucy asked, her crayon poised mid-air.

Sarah took a deep breath, setting down her fork. "I guess I am. At that town hall a year ago, I felt like I'd failed—not just my team but myself. I can still hear their voices, see their faces, how they looked at me… like I wasn't someone they could trust."

She paused, her throat tightening. "It was the worst day of my career. And now, standing in front of them again—no matter how much has changed—I can't help but wonder if I've done enough."

Alex reached across the table, placing a reassuring hand over hers. "Sarah, do you remember what you said to me that night? You told me you didn't know if you could fix it. And look at where you are now."

Sarah blinked, her eyes welling up. "But what if tomorrow reminds them of that moment? What if—"

"Mama, you're the best!" Lucy interrupted, her voice chirping with certainty. She held up her crayon drawing, a bright yellow sun with a smiling stick figure underneath it. "See? You make things better."

Sarah laughed softly, brushing away a tear. "Thanks, Lucy."

Alex leaned back in his chair, his tone firm but kind. "You've grown more this past year than in the decade I've known you. That town hall didn't define you—it pushed you to become the leader you are today. And you didn't just grow—you helped your team grow with you."

Sarah looked at him, her chest tightening. "But what if they still see the person who let them down?"

"They don't," Alex said firmly. "They see the person who listened to them, supported them, and brought out the best in them. Just like we do."

The weight in Sarah's chest began to lift. She looked at Lucy's drawing again, the joy radiating from the smiling sun. "Thanks, Lucy," she said, her voice steadying. "And thank you, Alex. I guess I needed to hear that."

"You've got this," Alex said with a small smile. "Tomorrow isn't about who you were a year ago—it's about who you are now."

Sarah nodded, a sense of calm beginning to replace her anxiety. Later that night, as she cleared the table and tucked Lucy into bed, her mind returned to Alex's words.

The town hall had been her breaking point, but it was also the moment that had set her on this path. Tomorrow wasn't just a test of how far she'd come—it was a celebration of what they had all built together.

Thursday, December 11, 10:00 AM – TechInnovate Headquarters, Townhall Meeting

"The Return to The Podium"

The morning air in the TechInnovate office hummed with energy. Employees moved briskly through the halls, their conversations laced with excitement about the annual day. The vibrant buzz around Sarah only made the weight in her chest feel heavier.

Clutching a slim folder, she adjusted her blazer and took a deep breath. The familiar route to the auditorium stretched before her, but every step felt heavier than it should. Her mind began replicating the memories she had tried hard to move past.

Her mind replayed the words that had cut through her like knives.

"Your team's delays are dragging us down."

The frustration in that voice still felt raw, as if it had been spoken yesterday.

"Do you even know what's causing the bottlenecks?"

The accusatory tone reverberated in her chest, making her breath catch.

Then came the blunt statement that had elicited laughter from the crowd:

LEVEL 10 LEADER

"Assurances don't deliver results."

The scattered laughter. The murmurs of agreement. The way her throat had tightened as she stood at the podium, unable to regain control of the room.

But it wasn't the audience's words alone that haunted her. It was the look she had seen in her team's eyes:

Karen's tight-lipped silence as she sat rigidly in her chair, her gaze fixed forward but her clenched jaw betraying her frustration.

Tom's restless shifting, his expression distant, his refusal to meet Sarah's eyes, as if he were searching for a way out of the discomfort.

Mia's furrowed brow and nervous glances around the room as if searching for reassurance that never came.

Those looks had spoken louder than any words. They hadn't just been hurt—they had felt betrayed. And Sarah had felt the full weight of that betrayal, even if it hadn't been her intention.

As she neared the auditorium's glass doors, another memory hit her: the empty desks and the eerie quiet of her workspace the day after the town hall.

Jessica's steady, measured words replayed in her mind: *"They feel that you exposed them in a way that was unprofessional and unfair."*

And Tom's devastating honesty during the apology meeting: *"The town hall was the worst day of my 20-year career."*

The weight of that statement settled over her again, the same guilt she had carried for months trying to resurface.

Sarah's steps faltered as she passed the conference room where she had faced her team after the town hall. The door was open, and for a brief moment, the scene played back in her mind with startling clarity.

The room had been stiflingly quiet that day, her team seated in tense silence. Karen's voice had been the first to cut through:

"It's not just about the town hall, Sarah. It's about feeling like you don't see us as a team."

Tom's words had been harsher, hitting like a blow:

"The town hall was the worst day of my 20-year career."

Sarah felt small, overwhelmed by the enormity of their disappointment. She stumbled through her apology, promising to rebuild her lost trust. But even as she left the room that day, she wondered, "Can I ever fix this?"

Walking past that room now, Sarah felt the same questions creep into her mind.

Have I done enough to rebuild their trust?

The past year had been full of effort—listening, learning, supporting. But was it enough?

Do they truly believe in me now?

Her team had grown—Karen had stepped into leadership, Tom had found purpose, and Mia blossomed confidently. But was their growth proof of her leadership or their resilience despite it?

As the auditorium's glass doors came into view, Sarah paused. Her reflection stared back at her, carrying the weight of everything she had worked for.

The hum of voices beyond the doors reminded her of what lay ahead. This wasn't just another event—it was her chance to face the people whose trust she had fought to rebuild.

LEVEL 10 LEADER

Taking a deep breath, she adjusted her blazer. She stepped forward, pushing the door open and walking into the auditorium's noise.

The auditorium buzzed with energy, applause punctuating the emcee's enthusiastic narration of the year's highlights. Employees cheered as milestones were announced, their excitement echoing through the expansive hall.

Sarah sat near the front, surrounded by her team. The warmth of the celebration should have been infectious, but her focus drifted. Her eyes caught on the stage—the polished wood and the sleek podium standing tall in the spotlight.

Her breath caught as her gaze lingered on it.

The image of herself standing at that very podium a year ago surged into her mind. She had clutched the edges of the lectern, her palms damp, her voice trembling as she delivered the numbers she knew would disappoint.

From that vantage point, the audience had been a sea of discontent.

She could still see the faces:

Ravi, the man in the back row, shook his head, his frown deepening as she stumbled through her explanations. His frustration had been palpable, his arms crossed in clear disapproval.

Sitting to the right, Priya scribbles furiously in her notebook, her pointed glances toward her neighbor filled with exasperation. Now and then, she nods sharply as though affirming her internal critique.

Jason, a few rows up, leaning toward his colleagues, whispers with an intensity that makes Sarah feel like every word is a critique aimed directly at her.

ANOTHER TOWNHALL

Her gaze shifted slightly, scanning the audience now. The same rows of chairs were filled with engaged employees, their faces lit with excitement as they cheered the company's achievements. Ravi sat near the back again, nodding as the emcee recounted a milestone. Priya smiled faintly as she clapped along with the others. Jason leaned back in his chair, looking relaxed and amused by the emcee's jokes.

This wasn't the same room it had been a year ago. But still, the podium seemed to loom, a reminder of the Sarah she had been—and the Sarah she hoped she had outgrown.

Her fingers tightened on the program in her lap. *Did they really see me differently now?*

She glanced at her team. Karen was clapping with the others, a faint smile on her lips. Tom leaned back in his chair, his posture relaxed, as he exchanged a joke with Mia. They looked at ease, but the question remained: *Have I truly rebuilt their trust—or have they just moved on despite me?*

The lights in the auditorium dimmed, drawing all attention to the stage as the emcee stepped back to the podium. Applause swept through the room, amplifying the excitement as the award ceremony officially commenced. The anticipation among the attendees was almost tangible. "Good afternoon, everyone!" the emcee said, their voices warm and engaging. It's my pleasure to kick off our annual awards segment, where we celebrate the incredible talent and dedication that drive TechInnovate forward."

The crowd erupted in cheers, but Sarah barely noticed. She sat stiffly in her chair, her hands gripping the edges of the program in her lap. Her heart was racing, and every word from the emcee seemed to drag.

The emcee continued, calling the first few award recipients to the stage. "And now, the Rising Star Award goes to... Mia!"

LEVEL 10 LEADER

Sarah's head snapped up at the mention of Mia's name, her team clapping loudly as Mia rose to accept the award. A faint smile crossed Sarah's lips as Mia made her way to the stage, but it faded quickly as her thoughts spiraled back inward.

The emcee's voice rang out over the applause as Mia returned to her seat, clutching her Rising Star Award. Sarah forced a smile as Mia sat down, her cheeks flushed with pride. Karen leaned over to whisper something encouraging, and Tom gave her a playful thumbs-up.

Sarah clapped, but her mind remained elsewhere—looping through memories of last year's town hall, her apology to the team, and the long journey to rebuild what she had lost. The warmth of the moment felt distant, barely touching her.

"And now," the emcee said, smiling warmly, "the next award celebrates leadership that inspires alignment, clarity, and focus. This year's Compass Award goes to... Karen!"

Sarah's head snapped up again as her team burst into applause. Karen froze momentarily, her eyes wide with surprise before she quickly composed herself and rose to her feet.

"Karen led cross-departmental alignment efforts during one of our most ambitious initiatives," the emcee continued. "Her ability to guide teams toward a shared vision has been instrumental in our success."

The applause swelled as Karen walked to the stage. Her movements were steady, but her expression betrayed a mix of pride and disbelief. Sarah watched her go, a faint smile tugging at her lips despite the storm brewing inside her.

Karen accepted the Compass Award, glancing briefly at the audience. "Thank you," she began, her voice clear but tinged with emotion. "This award is an honor, but it's not something I achieved alone. Alignment is about teamwork, and I've been lucky to work with some of the most incredible people. You know who you are."

She smiled, the faintest hint of a glance toward Sarah and the rest of the team before she stepped back from the microphone. The crowd erupted into applause as Karen returned to her seat, the trophy gleaming in her hands.

Sarah forced another smile as Karen sat down, but her hands tightened on the program in her lap. Watching Karen and Mia, recognized for their growth and contributions, should have filled her with pride. Instead, her mind circled back to the nagging doubts she couldn't shake.

Did I really help them get here? Or did they succeed despite me?

Her gaze drifted to the podium again, the memory of last year's disastrous town hall pulling her deeper into her thoughts. She remembered the weight of the audience's judgment, the sound of their laughter, and how her voice trembled as she tried to hold the room together.

Her breathing quickened slightly, and she glanced at Karen and Mia, who were now exchanging quiet congratulations. Karen's trophy glinted under the stage lights, a tangible reminder of their progress. *They're thriving. But am I?*

The emcee's voice called the next recipient to the stage, but Sarah barely registered the name. The applause felt distant, the voices around her muffled. She clenched the program tighter, the edges crumpling under her fingers.

How many more awards? she wondered, her chest tightening. *How much longer until this is over?*

Her gaze flicked to the stage again, her pulse quickening. *Am I ready to stand there again?*

LEVEL 10 LEADER

The emcee returned to the podium, their voice cutting through the applause that followed the last award. "And now, we come to one of the most meaningful awards of the evening. The *Great Coach Award* recognizes leadership that goes beyond achieving goals. It's about building trust, fostering growth, and inspiring others to reach their full potential."

The audience quieted, the weight of the moment settling over the room. The emcee continued, smiling warmly. "To present this award, I'd like to invite our Head of HR, John Williams, to the stage."

Sarah's heart skipped a beat. John. Her mind immediately flashed to the apology meeting. This measured, calm voice had spoken so firmly about the broken trust in her team. Her hands tightened around the edges of the program in her lap as John made his way to the podium.

The room erupted into applause as John stepped to the podium, the familiar presence of the Head of HR commanding the room. Sarah's heart pounded as she clutched the edges of the program in her lap, her breath shallow and her pulse quickening.

John adjusted the microphone, his voice steady and warm. "Good evening, everyone. The *Great Coach Award* is one of our most meaningful recognitions each year. It's about more than results—it's about leaders' impact on the people around them. It honors those who build trust, foster growth, and create environments where others can thrive."

He paused, letting the weight of his words settle over the audience. "What makes this award unique is how it's decided. This isn't a leadership team decision. It's entirely bottoms-up—nominated and voted on by those who experience that leadership daily."

ANOTHER TOWNHALL

The murmurs of interest and anticipation rippled through the room, but Sarah barely registered them. Her mind spun with questions. *Nominated by the people? Who could they have chosen?*

John's voice cut through her thoughts. "To help me present this award, I'd like to invite our CEO, Jessica Hale, to join me on stage."

The applause swelled as Jessica rose from her seat and made her way to the podium. Her smile was warm, but her presence radiated authority. Sarah's heart sank deeper into her chest as Jessica stood beside John, scanning the audience with her familiar, commanding gaze.

Jessica adjusted the microphone slightly, her voice clear and deliberate. "Thank you, John. The *Great Coach Award* holds a special place in my heart because it represents the essence of leadership—bringing out the best in others. It's about more than setting goals or achieving metrics. It's about creating a culture of trust, collaboration, and growth."

Her tone softened slightly as she continued. "This year's recipient embodies all of these qualities. They faced one of the most difficult challenges any leader can encounter: rebuilding trust after it was broken. But they didn't just rebuild—they redefined what it means to lead."

The room fell silent, and the anticipation was almost palpable. Jessica's eyes scanned the audience again, and her smile widened.

"This year's *Great Coach Award* goes to... Sarah Thompson."

The words hung in the air momentarily before the room erupted into applause.

Sarah froze, her breath catching as the name she least expected echoed in her ears. *Me?* she thought, her chest tightening. *They chose me?*

Beside her, Karen nudged her arm with a grin. "You heard her. Get up there!"

Mia clapped enthusiastically, her eyes bright with pride. Lisa reached over and gave Sarah's hand a reassuring squeeze while Tom leaned in with a quiet but firm, "You deserve this."

Slowly, Sarah rose to her feet. Her heart raced, and her legs were unsteady as she took her tentative steps toward the stage. The thunderous applause wrapped around her, but inside, she could still hear the doubt whispering. And yet, she walked forward — into the light.

At the steps to the stage, Sarah hesitated for a single breath. Then she straightened her blazer, took a deep inhale, and climbed.

Jessica and John waited at the top, their smiles calm and proud. Jessica stepped forward, voice warm but firm.

"Sarah, this moment is a testament to your leadership, resilience, and heart. A year ago, you stood on uncertain ground. You could have retreated, but instead, you chose to rise. You chose to listen. You chose to change. And in doing so, you didn't just rebuild trust — you created something stronger."

She turned to the audience. "This award, chosen by the people who work with Sarah daily, reflects the impact that transforms more than performance — it transforms culture. Sarah, you've shown us what leading with authenticity, humility, and courage means."

Jessica pulled her in for a brief but heartfelt hug. "You've earned this," she said softly.

John stepped forward and handed Sarah the sleek glass trophy. The lights caught the inscription:

ANOTHER TOWNHALL

> ## *"Great Coach Award - For Inspiring Growth and Transforming Culture."*

Sarah turned to face the audience, the award trembling slightly in her hands. Her team clapped the loudest—Karen wiping her eyes, Mia smiling through tears, Lisa beaming, and Tom nodding, jaw tight with pride.

She stepped toward the microphone. Her voice was soft but clear.

"Thank you," she said, steadying herself. "Jessica, John… and everyone here—thank you."

"This moment… this award… is something I never imagined a year ago. Back then, I wasn't even sure I belonged in this role. I had a team that didn't fully trust me—and truthfully, I didn't fully trust myself."

She paused, eyes sweeping the room.

"But more than anyone, this award belongs to my team."

She looked down at the first row.

"Karen, Mia, Tom, Lisa—you didn't just follow me. You walked beside me. You led beside me. And in many ways… you led *me*."

She turned to each of them.

"Karen—you were our compass. You aligned us when I couldn't find my own clarity. You grounded us in direction and integrity. You modeled grace under pressure."

LEVEL 10 LEADER

"Mia—you climbed with every challenge. I've watched you grow into a leader in your own right. You took risks, and you rose. You remind us what quiet strength really looks like."

"Tom—you held us together with purpose. You reminded us of *why* we do what we do. Your calm, clarity, and conviction gave this team its backbone."

"Lisa—you were the connector. You saw the patterns before anyone else. You helped us bridge gaps, anticipate challenges, and bring people along. You held the culture together through insight, empathy, and a fierce belief in what's possible."

Sarah's voice caught in her throat.

"You didn't just grow because of me—you grew despite me, especially in those early months when I didn't yet deserve the trust you gave me. You forgave me when I failed. You believed in me when I doubted myself. You gave me space to learn how to lead."

She exhaled, voice softer now. "This award isn't mine—it's *ours*."

She turned to the audience again, standing tall.

"And I can't accept this alone. Karen, Mia, Tom, Lisa—please join me on stage."

The room erupted into applause as the four stood.

Karen, still misty-eyed, walked with purpose. Mia followed, a steady smile on her face. Tom's stride was calm and confident. And Lisa—bright-eyed and proud—joined them with a nod and a hand on Sarah's shoulder as she reached the stage.

Sarah handed the award to Karen, who immediately pulled the rest of the team into a group embrace.

"This is for all of us," Sarah said quietly.

ANOTHER TOWNHALL

The audience rose to their feet, and the applause swelled into a thunderous standing ovation. The lights reflected off the trophy, casting long streaks of light across the walls.

Together, they stood shoulder to shoulder—Sarah, Karen, Mia, Tom, and Lisa—a united front—a living example of what transformation looks like when it's shared.

Sarah looked out over the crowd, then back at her team, her heart full.

Leadership isn't about standing ahead—it's about walking beside. It's about listening, growing, and rising together. Tonight, I know one thing for sure:

I didn't lead them—they led me.

Karen turned toward Sarah, leaning in with a quiet grin.

"I'm the second-happiest person in this room tonight."

Sarah laughed softly, tears finally spilling over. "Thank you, Karen."

Lisa wrapped her arm around Sarah's waist. "You're stuck with us now."

Mia smiled. "We're just getting started."

Tom gave a slow nod. "And the best part? We didn't win a title. We became a team."

And for the first time in a long time, Sarah didn't feel like she had to prove herself.

She felt at home.

Your Next Move

Was this chapter helpful?

If it sparked a new insight or gave you a practical tool, take 30 seconds to leave a quick review.

Your words might be the reason another leader takes the first step.

☞ Leave a review on Amazon

Ready to grow from a reader to a Level-10 Leader?

Unlock Level 10 Leadership Assessment, Workbook and more at resources.level10leader.com

RECAP

Every Great Journey Begins Somewhere

Every great leader starts somewhere. It began with a moment of doubt for Sarah—a town hall that left her questioning her abilities, purpose, and place as a leader. For you, it might have been stepping into a leadership role, facing a challenging team dynamic, or even deciding to pick up this book.

Leadership is never about perfection. It's about showing up—day after day—with courage, curiosity, and the willingness to learn. Through Sarah's story, you've seen how leadership isn't a straight path but a series of moments, decisions, and lessons that shape the leader and the people around them.

As you close this book, reflect on your journey. How far have you come? And where will you go next?

The Paradoxes of Leadership

Leadership is full of paradoxes. You've likely faced many of them already:

- **Be confident, but stay humble.**
- **Focus on people, but deliver results.**

- Drive clarity, but embrace uncertainty.
- Take responsibility, but empower others.

These contradictions aren't signs of failure—they're the reality of leadership. Sarah faced them, too, and she learned that the key isn't to solve these paradoxes but to navigate them with balance and intention.

The good news is you don't have to face these challenges alone.

The Power of Coaching

Sarah didn't transform overnight. She sought guidance. She reached out to Michael, a trusted mentor who challenged her to think differently, coached her through difficult moments, and helped her grow into the leader her team needed.

One of the most powerful lessons Sarah learned was that leadership isn't just about results—it's about relationships. Michael modeled this by meeting Sarah where she was, showing her the value of trust, and encouraging her to believe in herself.

Every leader needs a coach.

Whether it's a trusted colleague, a mentor, or even a professional coach, having someone who can offer perspective, support, and honest feedback is invaluable.

But coaching isn't a one-way street. As a leader, you have the opportunity—and responsibility—to coach others. Empower your team. Help them see their potential. Walk with them on their journey, just as someone has walked with you.

Ask yourself:

- *Who is coaching me?*
- *Who am I coaching?*

RECAP

The 10 Wins: A Framework for Leadership

This book has explored the **10 Wins Framework**, practical lessons that guide you through leadership challenges. Let's revisit them briefly:

Winning the Spirit

1. **Win with WHY:** Lead purposefully, driven by a clear understanding of your vision, values, and mission.

Winning the Heart

2. **Win with WHO:** Build strong, trusting relationships by understanding and connecting with your team members.

3. **Win with INCLUSION:** Foster a culture of inclusion where every team member feels seen, heard, and valued.
4. **Win with CAREERS:** Empower and support your team's professional growth, aligning their aspirations with organizational objectives.

Winning the Mind

5. **Win with GOALS:** Set clear, measurable goals that provide direction, focus, and drive for your team.
6. **Win with GROWTH:** Cultivate a growth mindset, fostering continuous learning and development within your team.
7. **Win with DELEGATION:** Distribute responsibilities effectively, empowering your team and building capacity.
8. **Win with FEEDBACK:** Create a feedback-rich culture where both giving and receiving feedback drive growth and improvement.
9. **Win with COACHING:** Empower your team to reach their full potential by adapting coaching styles to meet their unique needs.
10. **Win with REWARDS:** Celebrate successes and recognize contributions to foster motivation, engagement, and team morale.

Use these wins as a roadmap. Keep them close as you navigate the paradoxes of leadership.

RECAP

The Ripple Effect: Leadership Beyond Work

Leadership doesn't end when you leave the office. Sarah's journey wasn't just about her team—it was about her family, too.

As Sarah grew into her role as a leader, she found that the same skills—trust, resilience, and connection—strengthened her relationships at home. Her daughter Lucy saw a mom who faced challenges with courage and kindness. Her husband Alex watched her transform doubt into confidence, inspiring their family as much as her team.

Your growth as a leader can ripple into every part of your life. Stronger communication, greater empathy, and a renewed sense of purpose can make you a better manager, partner, parent, and friend.

A Final Thought: Leading with Purpose

Leadership is about more than managing tasks or achieving goals. It's about resilience, connection, and creating something bigger than yourself.

Sarah learned that the best leaders don't rise alone—they rise together.

So ask yourself: *What kind of leader do I want to be? How will I show up for my team, family, and myself?*

Remember, every step matters. Every moment counts. And every great leader starts somewhere—just like you.

Great Leaders aren't born; they choose to be coached into greatness!

AFTERWORD

A Journey of Growth and Gratitude

As you reach the final page of this book, I want to take a moment to share my deepest thanks.

This book follows the journey of Sarah, a new manager navigating the highs and lows of leadership. While Sarah is a fictional character, her experiences are drawn from real moments in my own life—moments of failure, learning, resilience, and transformation.

Michael and Jessica, Sarah's mentors, are reflections of the managers, mentors, and allies who believed in me even when I doubted myself. Their belief, especially in moments of darkness, changed the trajectory of my life and leadership. They are not just characters—they are tributes.

I also want to honor those who have walked beside me at every step:

To my father, Arun Kumar Tripathi, whose own journey as a best-selling author has inspired mine.

To my mother, Renuka Tripathi, for her unconditional love and the unwavering belief she instilled in me.

LEVEL 10 LEADER

To my wife, Shilpi—my strength, anchor, and greatest champion.

To my daughters, Anaya and Ira, who remind me every day that leadership begins at home.

To my siblings, Pragya, Akhil, and Dhruva, who always nudged me forward, especially when giving up felt easier.

To my mentors, colleagues, and friends—your guidance, honesty, and encouragement have helped shape the leader and human I strive to be. I am grateful beyond words.

To the Level 10 Leader publishing team—Tanmay, Shrishti, and Kanishka: Thank you for being the steady hands behind the scenes. This book is stronger, clearer, and more impactful because of each of you.

And, to you, the reader—thank you. You've invested your time in this journey, and I hope you leave with not just insights, but the courage to lead with clarity, purpose, and heart.

Let's continue this journey together.

With gratitude,
Nikhil Tripathi

Voices of Leadership

I had the privilege of working with Nikhil as one of his first associates. When we first met, he was an ambitious and idealistic young professional eager to innovate and reinvent processes almost daily. While his enthusiasm was inspiring, it often unsettled the team with its constant changes.

However, through continuous feedback grounded in reality, I witnessed an incredible transformation in Nikhil's leadership style. He evolved from an impatient, know-it-all manager into an inclusive team member, mentor, and caring leader. It's been a remarkable journey that I've had the honor of observing firsthand.

In *Level 10 Leader*, Nikhil distills his real-life experiences and the invaluable lessons he has learned. It is a treasure trove for aspiring and established leaders aiming to elevate their impact and effectiveness.

I wholeheartedly endorse *Level 10 Leader* for anyone leading or working within teams. A happy, engaged, and valued team can achieve truly exceptional results.

Mallika Anchan,
Ex. Senior Manager, Procter & Gamble

LEVEL 10 LEADER

Twenty years in a top corporate job have equipped Nikhil with all the tools to write this book with authority. Sarah's journey is bound to resonate with all of us; after all, which leader hasn't gone through this journey? We all have. Whether you are a new or an experienced leader, there is something in this book for everybody. And in a format that everybody loves – Storytelling! Enjoy the ride.

B.S. Ravishanker,
Retired Executive and Leadership Trainer, P&G and Infosys

By distilling his wealth of knowledge into actionable insights, Nikhil Tripathi has created a resource that resonates with authenticity and relevance. Whether you're a newcomer to the corporate world or a seasoned professional seeking to elevate your impact, *Level 10 Leader* provides a roadmap for navigating the intricacies of organizational life with confidence and purpose.

Bhavesh Shah,
Parallel Entrepreneur, and Ex. Chief Procurement Officer, Firmenich

"Nikhil Tripathi takes relatable organizational and leadership challenges and uses the powerful concept of Paradoxes as a tool to help young leaders understand what they're going through. He then helps them solve these dilemmas with practical tips. Principles and tips relevant not just for the corporate world, but for non-profits, other community organizations, and indeed, in our own lives. I wish Nikhil the very best of luck in this vital work to unlock purposeful leadership across organizations.

Rahul Malhotra,
Global Head of Brand Strategy & Stewardship, Shell

VOICES OF LEADERSHIP

Nikhil is one of the most caring leaders I've had the privilege to work with. His dedication to leveraging his team's strengths and supporting their development is truly inspiring. *Level 10 Leader* is a testament to his unique approach—offering people managers practical insights to build a coaching habit and foster inclusive, high-performing teams. It's a guide written with heart, spirit, and genuine care."

Richa Singh,
Podcast Host and Global Procurement Leader

About the Author

Nikhil Tripathi is a seasoned business leader with over 20 years of experience driving growth and organizational transformation across Asia and North America for a Fortune 50 corporation.

He rose from a humble family of teachers, freedom fighters, and farmers—an upbringing that instilled resilience, service, and a passion for lifelong learning.

With a background in engineering and an MBA, Nikhil built his career leading complex, fast-paced teams while discovering a deeper calling for coaching and people development. His leadership contributions have been recognized with honors such as the CEO Award, President Award, Master Trainer Award, and Great Coach Award.

Inspired by his father, Arun Kumar Tripathi, a best-selling author of six books, Nikhil wrote *Level 10 Leader*, a blend of storytelling, actionable insights, and research-backed strategies designed to help leaders grow and inspire others. The book is also a tribute to the mentors, managers, and associates who shaped his leadership journey.

Today, Nikhil lives in Cincinnati, Ohio, USA, with his wife Shilpi and daughters Ira and Anaya. Beyond his professional pursuits, he is fueled by a recently rediscovered life purpose: **to give, to grow, and to be grateful**—a compass guiding his ambition to impact **10 million lives over the next 10 years** through his writing, coaching, and leadership work.

Through Level 10 Leader and beyond, Nikhil hopes to inspire readers to embrace growth, lead with authenticity, and leave a legacy of trust, impact, and transformation.

Made in the USA
Monee, IL
15 September 2025

24706324R00184